Helmut Kussmann
Süllbreedenkamp 23
32479 Hille
Tel. 05703 / 31 67

Willy Russell
„Educating Rita"

19 Arbeitsblätter für einen handlungs- und
produktionsorientierten Literaturunterricht

D1640103

Willy Russell
„Educating Rita"

19 Arbeitsblätter für einen handlungs- und
produktionsorientierten Literaturunterricht

Willy Russell
„Educating Rita"

19 Arbeitsblätter
für einen handlungs- und produktionsorientierten Literaturunterricht

von Detlef und Margaret von Ziegésar

Ernst Klett Verlag
Stuttgart Düsseldorf Leipzig

Textausgaben:

Willy Russell, Educating Rita. Edited and annotated by A.-R. Glaap. Diesterweg 1997.
Willy Russell, Educating Rita. Longman Literature 1991.
Die Seitenverweise dieses Heftes beziehen sich auf die Diesterweg-Ausgabe.

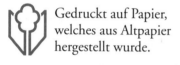 Gedruckt auf Papier,
welches aus Altpapier
hergestellt wurde.

Die Deutsche Bibliothek – CIP-Einheitsaufnahme

Ziegésar, Detlef von:
Willy Russell, „Educating Rita" : 19 Arbeitsblätter für ein
handlungs- und produktionsorientierten Literaturunterricht /
von Detlef und Margaret von Ziegésar. – 2. Aufl. –
Stuttgart ; Düsseldorf ; Leipzig : Klett, 1998
    ISBN 3-12-927893-1

2. Auflage 1998
Alle Rechte vorbehalten
© Ernst Klett Verlag GmbH, Stuttgart 1997
Internetadresse: http://www.klett.de
Umschlaggestaltung: BSS Werbeagentur Sachse und Partner, Bietigheim
DTP: Kirsten Brückmann, Stuttgart
Repro: Windhueter, Schorndorf
Druck: Wilhelm Röck, Weinsberg. Printed in Germany.
ISBN 3-12-927893-1

Contents

Introduction

This collection of worksheets is intended for grades 11 – 13 of the grammar school ("Grundkurse" and "Leistungskurse"). The 19 worksheets, together with teaching hints and answers, form a coherent course covering the most important aspects of Willy Russell's play *Educating Rita*. Alternatively, the worksheets can be used individually to supplement other material. Since Russell's drama has often been compared to George Bernard Shaw's *Pygmalion*, a comparison between the two plays is included at the end of the interpretation. Suggestions are also made for incorporating video clips from the film *Educating Rita*, the script of which was written by Russell himself. Including these video clips, the course will take approximately 20 forty-five-minute lessons.

The play touches on topics which are close to the students' own experience, such as the role of women, the link between education and social class, and the mass media.

Authentic texts interspersed throughout the interpretation provide useful background information on modern Britain and also about Russell himself and his role in modern British theatre.

Approaching literature

Literary critics and researchers on the reading process postulate the following two opposing models of how people read and interpret texts in general and literary texts in particular:

– reading and interpreting as the uncovering of already existing meaning;
– reading and interpreting as the creation of something new and personal by the reader.

We do not see these two positions as mutually exclusive, but rather as the two extremes of a continuum along which readers move freely, at times discovering meaning within the text and at times creating their own personal meaning. As a consequence, the tasks in this course cover the whole spectrum of response: some are oriented towards the knowledge and experience which learners bring to bear on the text, others focus more on detailed text analysis.

A personal, creative response to the text is encouraged by tasks such as speculating about characters and events, making predictions, extending and inventing dialogues or altering parts of the text. Involving students personally also gives them the insight that the same text can be interpreted differently by different people. Learner-centred tasks of this kind especially lend themselves to pair and group work, which requires students to argue their points, back arguments up with evidence and reflect about their own norms and values.

The tasks are also designed to furnish students with a set of analytic tools for approaching drama in general, covering questions such as the playwright's intention, relevant autobiographical elements, the historical and literary context, themes, genre, characters, setting, plot, dialogue and language.

One recurrent pedagogical question when teaching literature is whether the text should be read at one go or split into smaller sections. The latter approach has been selected for this course since it has the following advantages:

– students are not overfaced;
– it prevents the accumulation of misunderstandings and subjective, unfounded interpretations;
– it provides more opportunities for communicative and creative language work;
– the students' curiosity about further developments can be sustained.

The film version of *Educating Rita*

Another question is whether to take the film version of the play into account or not. We feel it should be included, since dramas are meant to be performed. Furthermore, students should realise that plays exist both as literary texts and as theatre performances. If students have no access to a theatre production, then the next best thing is the film version, particularly if it sticks closely to the original, as does *Educating Rita*.

The incorporation of the video has the following advantages:

– The additional information in the film about Rita's home life and relationship with her husband and family helps students to understand her predicament. The contrast between working and middle class culture becomes more obvious.

5

- The film gives information about working class life in general in a northern English city like Liverpool.
- The changes in Rita's appearance are only shown in the film.
- Characters who are only briefly referred to in the text, such as Denny and Trish, gain more depth. We also see more of Frank's private life.
- The accompanying gestures, facial expressions, tone of voice and background information facilitate understanding, provide models for the students' own language production and sensitise them to the role of these features in the communication process.
- Generally speaking, films provoke a more spontaneous response than texts and have a more emotional impact. It would be a pity not to exploit this potential for encouraging students to express their own feelings and ideas.
- The film is very useful for language exercises such as listening comprehension and descriptions of characters, settings, atmosphere and events.

In this course video clips do not serve as rewards for successful work on the text, but are an integral part of the whole interpretation. Film scenes are used for general comprehension, whilst the written text is preferred for more differentiated discussions entailing textual references. However, since it is not always possible to incorporate the film version of *Educating Rita*, the course is designed for use either with or without the video.

Besides contributing to the understanding of the drama, the course also aims at giving students the confidence to develop, express, value and question their own responses to the work. At the same time they improve their skills in the fields of reading, writing, listening and speaking.

1. The story

Here are some quotations from the play we are going to read, but all except the first one are in the wrong order. Try to put them into the correct order so that you can imagine what the story will be about. What sort of people do you imagine Frank and Rita are?

1. FRANK: ... why did you enrol in the first place?
    RITA: Because I wanna know.
2. FRANK: Possessing a hungry mind is not, in itself, a guarantee of success.
3. FRANK: There is a way of answering examination questions that is expected... And you must observe those rules.
4. RITA: ... he's wonderin' where the girl he married has gone to.
5. RITA: He said either I stop comin' here an' come off the pill or I could get out altogether.
6. RITA: I want to change.
7. RITA: What's up, Frank, don't y' like me now that the little girl's grown up...? I'm educated, I've got what you have an' y' don't like it because you'd rather see me as the peasant I once was.
8. RITA: I've been realizin' for ages that I was, y' know, slightly out of step. I'm twenty-six. I should have had a baby by now; everyone expects it... I wanna discover meself first. Do you understand that?
    FRANK: Yes.
    RITA: Yeh. They wouldn't round our way.
9. RITA: What I learn from you, about art an' literature, it feeds me, inside... Denny tried to stop me comin' tonight... They hate it when one of them breaks away.
10. FRANK: If you're going to... pass examinations you're going to have to suppress, perhaps even abandon your uniqueness. I'm going to have to change you.
11. RITA: ... y' sit there, don't y', watchin' the ballet or the opera on the telly an' – an' y' call it rubbish cos that's what it looks like? Cos y' don't understand.
12. RITA: I don't need you to hold my hand as much... don't keep treatin' me as though I'm the same as when I first walked in here.
13. RITA: Comin' here, doin' this, it's given me more life than I've had in years.
14. RITA: My mind's full of junk, isn't it? It needs a good clearin' out.

What else would you like to know about the story? Write down your questions and check if they are answered as you get to know the play.

1. The beginning – Starting with the video

What do we learn from this video clip about the story and about this man?

2. First impressions: Frank

Read pages 7–10 up to 1.8 (…erotic). Then look at the phone call on p. 8 in detail. From this phone call and the accompanying stage directions give your first impressions of Frank. Put the relevant quotations in this table and write down your conclusions in note form.

Quotations	Conclusions
– He manages … receiver –	

Make up the whole phone call, including what the caller says. First you take the part of Frank and your partner is the caller. Then exchange roles and do it again.

3. Rita

Do you think this girl, Rita, is a normal student? Why do you think she has come to the university?
Does this information give you a clue as to why Rita is here?

Studying with the Open University

The Open University has become one of the great success stories of British education. It is the largest and most innovative university in the UK, with a world-wide reputation for the quality of its courses and the effectiveness of its methods. More than two and a half million people have already studied with us – on average 200 000 people annually in recent years – so what makes the Open University so special?

- The Open University (OU) is the university that comes to you. Wherever you live, the courses you take will have the same high quality content and will be taught to the same high standards.
- The OU is genuinely open. There are no entry qualifications (except for higher degrees), no admission interviews, no barriers of any kind. As long as you are over 18, normally resident in the UK or elsewhere in the European Union and want to study, we will accept you, as soon as a place is available on your chosen course.
- The OU is flexible. You can tailor your studies to fit in with the rest of your life. You don't need to take time off work or give up your social life completely! Indeed, 75% of OU students remain in full-time employment throughout their studies.

The Open University offers four main types of study.

Single courses

If you study one of the University's courses you will be attached to a tutor and will be expected to produce regular written work. In many cases there is also an end of course examination.

When you register for an Open University course you do not commit yourself to further study. It is up to you whether you go on to complete a qualification and, even if you do, you can take a break between courses. Many people study only one or two courses, to acquire new skills or update their knowledge in areas relevant to their work or other interests. Others study for intellectual satisfaction or simply for enjoyment. All the courses listed in this brochure can be studied singly and most can be accumulated to-wards a qualification.

Read the extracts from the information brochure again to find out:

– if you need to take an entrance examination to start studying at the Open University.
– if students have to study full-time; what do they do if they have jobs?
– Is the Open University only for British people?
– How are students taught?

If the woman in the video is a new student, what kind of course do you think she will have chosen and why? How do you think she will relate to the lecturer?

(Brochure: Studying with the Open University. The Open University, Milton Keynes 1996)

4. Rita's entrance

Think of the way Rita came into Frank's study. Is this how a new student would normally come into the room of a lecturer she had not met before? Rewrite her entrance in a more conventional way.

FRANK: *Come in! Come in!*
RITA: *...?*

How does Frank react to Rita's entrance? What would he have expected? What conclusions can you draw about Rita's personality and her background?

5. 'Normal' universities

Compare Frank's and Rita's descriptions of how the Open University differs from 'proper' universities (p. 10).

	Rita	Frank
'normal' university		
The Open University		

6. A new student

A 'mature student', aged 23, has just begun studying at
St Katherine's College of Education in Liverpool. He is being
interviewed by one of the officials there. From his replies,
deduce what questions the interviewer asked.

> INTERVIEWER: …?
> STUDENT: In 1947, in Whiston, just outside Liverpool.
> INTERVIEWER: …?
> STUDENT: Fifteen.
> INTERVIEWER: …?
> STUDENT: Secondary school.
> INTERVIEWER: …?
> STUDENT: No, not at all. I wasn't interested, you see. The only thing I enjoyed was the reading lessons. That's when I first started thinking I might become a writer myself.
> INTERVIEWER: …?
> STUDENT: Well, there were lots of discussions, even rows, about what I should do. And eventually my mother said I should become a ladies' hairdresser. So I did.
> INTERVIEWER: …?
> STUDENT: Six years. When we weren't too busy I read. But eventually I decided that if I was really going to become a writer I would have to do something about it.
> INTERVIEWER: …?
> STUDENT: Well, I realized that I needed to be among the kind of people who would understand, that I would have to move into the academic world.
> INTERVIEWER: …?
> STUDENT: No, it wasn't an easy one at all. Because I had to leave the kind of people, the kind of environment I had grown up in. I knew people wouldn't understand, that they'd be hurt.
> INTERVIEWER: …?
> STUDENT: I decided to become a student. That way I would be able to learn a job. And I'd have time to do some writing.
> INTERVIEWER: …?
> STUDENT: No, I didn't. And I couldn't go to night school to get them because it would have taken too long. I had to find a full-time course. But first I had to earn the money to pay for it.
> INTERVIEWER: …?
> STUDENT: I took a night-shift job in a factory, cleaning oil from the girders high above the machinery. It was very dangerous, but the money was good. As soon as I had enough I stopped and enrolled here as a student.

Can you guess the student's name?

1. 'Good' poetry

In an interview Willy Russell explained what he thinks about people who teach and analyse literature.

> "There's something I call the "literature industry" which has sprung up and which I particularly loathe because it seems to me to put a huge barrier between the Ritas of this world who want to learn and literature itself. It probably comes out in my own sort of situation; for years and years and years I wouldn't pick a classical or known and regarded author from the bookshelves. I'd rather read a racy, accessible American novel or indeed quality American novels because they were rarely classified as literature... (I'm) trying to attack the divisions really in teaching, in education, and in the class system. And so it's the division and it's the elitist way in which literature is dealt with that I really object to."

(Interview with Russell in: Glaap, A.-R.: Educating Rita. Comments and Study Aids. Diesterweg, Frankfurt 1984, S. 21)

Compare Russell's feelings with Rita's comment on poetry on p. 11, l.22. Have you ever felt like this? What could she be saying about people who teach literature?

a) They love literature for its own sake. ☐

b) They see literature as a means of gaining social prestige. ☐

c) They will read any kind of literature. ☐

d) They prefer literature which is difficult to understand. ☐

e) They think that if they classify literature which is difficult to understand as 'good', they will seem clever. ☐

2. Tell me what you watch and I'll tell you who you are

Look at Rita's remarks on the kind of TV programmes people from her background watch (p. 12). Circle what you think they would watch. Which programmes people like Frank would prefer?

TV Saturday March 22			
BBC 1	**BBC 2**	**ITV** Granada	**Channel 4**
6.15 The New Adventures Of Super man	6.00 The Cosby Show	6.00 Sesame Street	7.00 A Week In Politics Witty and informed guide to events at Westminster, with Andrew Rawnsley and Vincent Hanna. Including News and Weather.
7.50 The National Lottery Live	7.05 News; Weather.	6.40 Regional News	
9.00 The Outer Limits Sci-fi/horror	8.00 **Preview** The Goldring Audit: Marx Goldring looks at the Common Agricultural Policy	6.45 News; Weather	
11.15 Newsnight	9.30 **Film** A Tale Of Two Cities (Ralph Thomas, 1958) British drama based on the Dickens classic.	7.30 A Lesson For Us All Second half the documentary on educational failure. Are we asking too much of teachers?	9.00 News; Weather
12.20 **Film** Crossplot (Alvin Rakoff, 1969) Thriller in which the answers are to be found in a half-finished crossword puzzle. See Movie Preview.	11.15 **Film** Kramer vs Kramer (Robert Benton, 1979) Multi-Oscar-winning drama about marital breakdown	8.40 The Money Programme Reporting on financial and economic issues.	9.15 Richard II Deborah Warner directed this TV version of her acclaimed production of Shakespeare's drama of power and treachery.
1.55 Weather	12.00 The Midnight Hour	9.30 **Film** Fletch Lives (Michael Ritchie, 1989) Comedy starring Chevy Chase	10.30 Under The Influence News series on the Church's impact on British culture.
2.00 Close	12.30 Learning Zone: Open University: The Lyonnais – A Changing Economy	10.55 News; Weather	12.15 The Sky At Night
	1.30 Modern Art	11.10 Regional News	2.10 Weather
	1.50 Close	12.45 Weather	2.15 Close
		2.50 Close	

11

3. Rita's environment

How does Rita feel about the people she meets? Does she blame them for the way they behave? Why does she sometimes hate them?
If you were an artist, what kind of picture would you draw or paint to show how Rita feels? Have you ever felt like that?

4. Rita's needs

Look at these descriptions of courses similar to the ones Rita has enrolled for. How do they explain what she means when she says, 'I wanna know' (p. 12) and 'what's it like to be free?' (p. 13). Freedom from what, to do what?
How do you think her family and friends will react to her studies?

LITERATURE	
A210	Approaching literature: authors, readers, texts
A319	Literature in the modern world

ART HISTORY	
A316	Modern art: practices and debates
A354	Art, society and religion in Siena, Florence and Padua, 1280–1400

Approaching literature: authors, readers, texts   **A210**

How do we work out what a text means? How does a play move from the page into performance? The course tackles such questions through study of a variety of texts. In *The realist novel* you will study four well-known nineteenth-century novels. Then, through writers such as Louisa May Alcott, Alice Walker and Henryk Ibsen, you will explore the relationship between *literature and gender*. In *Shakespeare, Aphra Behn and the canon* Shakespeare is studied alongside the first important woman playwright. Finally in *Romantic writings* some of the greatest English poetry is set in the politics and culture of its time.

60	2	A	£ 357

Literature in the modern world   **A319**

Reading modern literature with greater knowledge and awareness is at the heart of this course.

('Courses, Diplomas and BA/BSc Degrees'. The Open University, Milton Keynes 1997)

Does 'freedom' mean the same to you as it does to Rita? Write down a few words which you associate with 'freedom'.

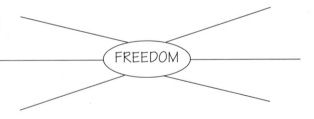

5. Highbrow and lowbrow literature

Read on to the end of the scene and list the authors which Frank and Rita know. Find out what kind of things they wrote.
Do you think Rita would be able to pass an exam on English

1. Elite culture, popular culture

Collect evidence from the first scene to show whether Rita or
Frank is more conscious of the class differences between them.
Which of them is more aware of social class altogether?
Using the following definition of 'culture' make a table showing
the differences between elite tastes and popular or mass culture,
as far as the arts are concerned.

When the term *culture* is used in connection with the arts, it
is often used to describe certain kinds of arts (so-called elite
arts, which make up elite culture) – opera, ballet, "serious"
poetry and novels, symphonic music, and other arts that
require of audiences, generally speaking, elevated and
educated tastes and refined sensibilities. People who go to
symphonies, read classic novels, and attend the ballet, for
example, are often described in popular parlance as "cultured".
This would suggest, of course, that people who do not like
these arts (but like what have been called the popular arts, the
public arts, and mass culture) are "uncultured" or without
culture, which is absurd.

There is, then, another kind of culture, which we call
popular culture, a term generally used to describe such things
as comic strips, most television programs and radio shows,
formulaic[1] novels (such as romances, detective novels, and
science fiction novels), popular music (rock, rap, country-
western, and so on), fashions, fads, and sports. That is, popular
culture is made up of mass-mediated culture and other related
aspects of culture that are generally consumed by large
numbers of people on a continual basis.

Sometimes it is difficult to say where works of popular art
stop being popular and become elite, or vice versa. If
Shakespeare's *Hamlet* is broadcast on television, does it
become popular culture?

(...)

Even people who like the elite arts may also have a taste for
popular culture. Many people who might go to the symphony
on Friday night would also enjoy a football game on Saturday
afternoon, or who read "serious" novels during the day like to
watch situation comedies, action-adventure shows, or the like
at night.

(Reprinted by permission of Sage
Publications Ltd. from Arthur Asa
Berger: Cultural Criticism, London
1995, pp. 137–138)

[1] written to a formula, which is always the same

Elite culture	Popular culture

Compare the tastes of people like Rita and Frank with your
table.

2. There's 'talking' and 'talkin'

It has been suggested that the working class, especially the lower
working class, have a completely different way of speaking to the
middle class, a different 'code'. Decide in how far this theory
applies to Frank and Rita. Look in particular at their
conversation on p. 17, l.28 – p. 18, l.3 (Well… honest).

Bernstein argues that the
lower working class
typically speaks a **"public"** or
"restricted" language; with
simple grammar, sentences
often unfinished, poor syntactical form and little use of
impersonal categories such as
"one". The middle classes, on
the other hand, use a **"formal"**
or **"elaborated"** code,
characterized by a more
complex grammatical and
syntactical form, a more
extensive vocabulary, and so
on. While there are enormous
problems in isolating and
classifying these differences,
they have special significance
in the case of the working-class
child's encounters with the
educational system…
The working-class child is less
able to express his own
particular response to situations, because he relies heavily
on standardized sayings within
his community, such as
proverbs; also he is less capable
of expressing his feelings in
detail because he has a more
restricted vocabulary than the
middle-class child. Since most
schools are dominated by
(middle-class) teachers using
the **"formal"** or **"elaborated"**
speech code, the working-class
child suffers from the handicap
of having to learn these speech
patterns in order to qualify for
social and academic approval.

(E.A. Johns: The Social Structure of Modern Britain, 1979, pp. 181–183, with permission from Elsevier Science Ltd., The
Boulevard, Langford Lane, Kidlington OX5 1GB, UK)

What important conclusion does Bernstein draw?
If you were a teacher how would you try to improve this
situation?

Fill in this table with examples from the exchange on p. 17/18:

	Frank	Rita
Type of sentences	–	–
Hesitation (fillers)		
Repetition		
Pronunciation		
Vocabulary		

3. 'Translating' Rita's speech

'Translate' what Rita said on p. 18 into the middle class code used by people like Frank.

4. Frank, an acceptable teacher?

Can you see a link between the two different speech codes and Rita's 'testing' of Frank (p. 13)?
What kind of person did she probably expect? Why do you think she likes Frank?
The meeting could have turned out differently. Think of what might have happened:

– If Frank had ..., Rita/she ...
– Rita can only accept a teacher who ...

Have you ever felt rejected because of the kind of language you use?

5. Out of step

On p. 18 Rita tells Frank that she feels 'out of step' with her environment (as if she were dancing to a different tune). Explain what she means with regard to her family, her husband, the neighbours and her customers.
How do Rita's comments about her customers underline her own actions?
What do you think about Rita's changing her name (p. 15)?

6. Rita and Frank – a paradox

How do you think Rita and Frank would complete these sentences? Can you see a paradox?

Rita: My life is ... I feel ... To me, Frank represents ...
Frank: My life is ... I feel ... To me, Rita represents ...

7. A breath of fresh air

After Rita leaves Frank goes to the pub, where he tells a friend about her. Explain how he felt about her when she first came into his study and how his attitude gradually changed.

"Do you know, a breath of fresh air came into my room today for the first time in years. You see, I've taken on an Open University course and ..."

1. Public schools

Rita tells Frank that she would have liked to go to a public school (pp. 22–23). Circle the things in the following advertisements which would have attracted Rita. What would probably have prevented her from going to one?

At Croft House individual care and guidance in a friendly family community is at the heart of our philosophy. We aim to help each girl to achieve her full potential, which can be academic success, or success in artistic, athletic or practical areas.

Our aim is that girls should leave us equipped to lead happy purposeful lives, and be able to accept responsibility and contribute to the community.

CROFT HOUSE

We offer:

- High academic standards
- A broad and flexible curriculum
- Our own stables and indoor riding school
- Wide variety of extra curricular and weekend activities
- Escorts to and from airports
- Guardians arranged
- Recognised by the Department of Education

 Cheltenham College
Junior School
Independent Co-educational School
First class boarding education
Caring environment
Parkland setting in Cheltenham
Superb facilities
Main entry at 7 and 11
Good transport links to major airports

KINGHAM HILL SCHOOL
The Boarding Experts
Girls & Boys 11–18 (98% Boarders)
Full boarding with activities 7 days a week
Small classes allowing for individual attention
Small, family run boarding houses
A very successful Dyslexia Department
KINGHAM HILL SCHOOL
Kingham, Chipping Norton Oxon OX7 6TH
United Kingdom

Still, the wealthiest of the British elite continue sending their offspring to upper crust fee-paying boarding schools. These oldest and most elite institutions, with legendary names like Eton and Harrow – are still flourishing despite spiraling costs. In fact, many parents may see higher fees – which can reach up to £ 14,000 ($ 21,500), as a social filter to separate those who can afford it from those who can't…

(The Christian Science Monitor, January 5–11, 1996)

Daily Mail, Wednesday, September 6, 1995   Page 3

AND DON'T FORGET YOUR PEN ... WILLIAM'S £ 5,537 CHECKLIST AT HIS NEW SCHOOL

Kitted out for Eton

PRINCE William starts at Eton today ... and his first lesson will be in handling the media.

More than 200 television cameramen, photographers and reporters from all over the world are expected to converge on the Berkshire public school for a photo-call authorised by Buckingham Palace.

But from there on in, the British Press has agreed to leave the 13-year-old royal pupil in peace as he settles in as a boarder at Manor House – his term-time home for the next five years.

Like many of the other 200 Eton new boys – on what is a nerve-racking occasion for any youngster – the Prince will be accompanied today by his parents. Brother Harry will also be there to help ease the pressures. William will be known as Prince William, or William Wales, in class and be referred to as plain William on informal occasions at Manor House.

During his first few days, he will be getting used to wearing the Eton uniform and sorting out the array of dress items and equipment required at the school – from collar studs and tailcoats to a tuck box and ottoman for his room.

But, as you would expect, nothing at Britain's most prestigious educational establishment comes cheap. The Daily Mail calculates that the cost of setting William in is £ 5,537.66–£ 1,862.57 for his uniform and sports kit, plus £ 3,675.09 for items he will need in his room. On top of that, of course, are the school's fees of £ 12,500 a year.

By contrast, new boys going to a local comprehensive, Windsor Boys School, can be kitted out with uniform and sports gear for a modest £ 221.86.

So what will the Pupil Prince be taking with him to Eton? Here, the Mall takes a look at the royal shopping list.

ITEM BY ITEM, HOW IT ADDS UP

Two tailsuits	£ 360
Chair	£ 1,195
Duvet, sheets, tablecloths	£ 200
Lampshade	£ 54.50
Stool	£ 29.95
Bin	£ 24
Underwear	£ 44.40
Two dark pullovers	£ 26.25
Six white tunic shirts	£ 82.50
Three pyjamas	£ 44.25
Footwear	£ 244.75
Socks	£ 39.95
Swimming trunks	£ 5.65
Two sportshirts	£ 37
Two pairs shorts	£ 29.50

Tuck box	£ 49.95
The Ottoman	£ 440
Shoe-cleaning kit	£ 13.75
Toilet bag	£ 10
Braces / cufflinks	£ 40.95
Lamps	£ 37
Towels and brushes	£ 57.25
Tracksuit	£ 45
Overnight bag	£ 45
Mug/handkerchiefs	£ 17.90
Raincoat	£ 124.95
Dressing gown	£ 28
Trousers	£ 45
Sports jacket	£ 75
Six stiff collars	£ 28.85

THIS is the basic list of items required by an Eton new boy. William will need additional clothes, plus equipment for his room – such as carpets, lights and curtains – which bring the likely total outlay to £ 5,537

2. Frank and public schools

When Rita tells Frank that she always dreamed of attending a public school his reply is cynical, 'God forbid it, why?' Can you imagine his reasons? Would you have liked to go to a public school?

17

1. Rita's school days

Pick out the passage in scene 2 which reflects the ideas in this extract from a newspaper article about a very intelligent girl's life at school.

"Our daughter was profoundly unhappy," her mother said.

"She felt she was being rejected by a group of her peers. Despite her and our best efforts, the group persisted in being extremely cliquey, arrogant – and pushed her out. Her whole world revolved around this clique."

(The Sunday Times, 14 April 1996: Bullies mar school for bright children)

How would Rita have finished these sentences?

a) If I had worked hard at school...

b) Where I lived you were not allowed...

c) All my friends expected me...

d) They did not expect me...

2. Girls and school

What other reasons for Rita's failure at school are suggested by this song?

When I went to school I learned to
    write and how to read,
Some history, geography and
    home economy,
And typing is a skill that every girl
    is sure to need,
To while away the extra time until
    the time to breed,
And then they had the nerve to
    say, 'What would you like to be?'
I says, 'I'm gonna be an engineer!'

NO, YOU ONLY NEED TO LEARN TO
    BE A LADY
THE DUTY ISN'T YOURS, FOR TO
    TRY AND RUN THE WORLD,
AN ENGINEER COULD NEVER HAVE
    A BABY,
REMEMBER, DEAR, THAT YOU'RE A
    GIRL.

(Adams/Laurikietietis: The Gender Trap. Quartet Books, London 1976, p. 16)

3. School and real life

Rita tells Frank about the incident with the beautiful bird (p. 28, ll. 22–31). Draw lines to show which of these words Rita would associate with school and which with real life. Can you add some of your own?

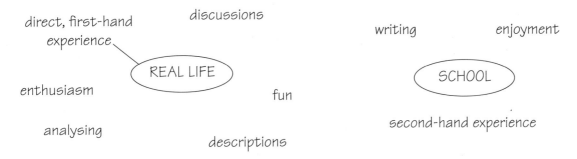

Look at Frank's reaction '(sighing) … education'. What does he seem to be saying? Do you agree? Should teaching methods be changed?

4. Analysing literature

Compare Rita's approach to literature with the more academic 'literary appreciation' which Frank expects from students of literature.

Frank	Rita
Students of literature should…	Literature should…
Literature need not…	Literary appreciation is based on…

Do you think Rita will succeed in learning the accepted methods of literary criticism? Do you see any danger in her learning to think like Frank and his students?
How do you feel when you are asked to give a considered opinion on literature or on a piece of music you like?

5. Frank

What do we learn about Frank from the conversation on pp. 26, l.20 – p. 29, l.16?

1. Housing

The following text deals with different types of housing in Britain. Where would you place Rita and Denny on this ladder? What type of house do you think Frank lives in? (Remember the conversation in scene one).

The Housing Ladder

English people see the housing market as a *ladder* (...), so they worry about where they live a great deal. At the bottom are starter homes, flats or tiny houses built as cheaply as possible to enable the first-time buyer to get his foot on that vital first rung of the ladder. If the market is functioning normally and the owners are doing reasonably well at work, it will only be a couple of years before they start looking round for something a little larger and a little more attractive. They may genuinely need more room because a baby is on the way, but this will hardly ever be the only reason for a move. Above (most) flats on the housing ladder, and also above terraced houses, comes the archetypal British "semi". These are the houses built in mirror-image pairs which you can see on the approach roads to nearly every town or city. They vary in size and status depending on when and where they were built. A big, old semi in a quiet and leafy suburb will enjoy much higher status than a small, boxy detached house nearly touching its neighbour on a new housing estate (...)

Most houses have a garden. We expect to be able to enter and leave our dwellings at ground level via a path and a bit of grass. The feeling that this is the way things ought to be is probably the reason why flats have never really caught on in England (...)

Doing little jobs around the house and garden competes with television as the main leisure activity in England. No newspaper is complete without its gardening column, in cartoon form in some of the tabloids. Millions of pounds are spent at gardening centres (which are often like plant hypermarkets) and DIY supermarkets.

(Speight, Stephen: Understanding England. EngLang Books, Southampton 1996, pp. 81–82)

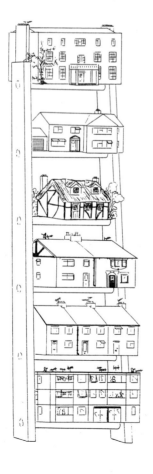

6. Mansion/Villa/Castle

5. Detached house

4. Cottage

3. Semi-detached house

2. Terraced house

1. Council flat

2. Interrupting Rita

Rita's husband likes making improvements to the house. Often these are very noisy, so that Rita cannot work properly. But there are also other difficulties. One week Rita does not manage to do her homework because other people keep interrupting her. She writes a note to Frank to explain. Can you imagine what the interruptions were?

> Dear Frank,
> I'm sorry I couldn't do this week's homework.
> You see,

a neighbour

my mother

I had to

wanted me to

needed help with

my sister's getting married and she

1. How to write literary criticism

a) Frank is not very happy with Rita's essay on *Howards End*. Why not? Remember what you have been taught about writing essays on literature. Make a list of conventions for writing them which would help someone like Rita.

b) Do you think Rita will ever be able to write an orthodox essay on a piece of literature?

c) What does Rita still have to learn?

2. How do you tell?

In scene 3 Rita asks Frank how you can tell which books are regarded as 'literature' (p. 31, l. 31). This confuses and embarrasses him. Could you have given her an answer? If you wanted to write a best-seller, what would you put into it?

3. Russell on 'good' literature

In an interview Russell himself commented on Rita's question 'How do you tell?' (p. 31, l. 34). List the people he holds responsible for propagating a 'high art culture'. What do these people think about art?

> RUSSELL: (…) it would be better if you didn't have a high art culture and a polarized working-class culture.
>
> JONES: (…) I know, for example, that Rita reads the wrong books and she asks Frank…
>
> RUSSELL: How do you tell literature, yes.
>
> JONES: His response is…
>
> RUSSELL: One's always known, really, yes.
>
> JONES: There is a plea in there, is there not, for a removal of those barriers?
>
> RUSSELL: Yes. The writers of those original works do not set up those barriers, because any writer, no matter what the form is he's working in, any writer worth his salt, is trying to reach everybody. But we do have a literature industry, an opera industry, a theatre industry, and the spokesmen are generally people who think that art is only for the few and reinforce that view from time to time (…) The shapers, the makers, of the stranglehold are the writers *about* it, the communicators *about* it, not the communicators themselves. I know for example when first I wanted to write drama, I diligently read *Theatre Quarterly* and *Drama Magazine*. I could feel all the time being pulled into one approved direction, one approved style. There was a Michael Radcliffe piece in *The Observer* that presents us with what he thinks we should go and see. And he wants us to be guilty about going to see what we do see.

(Jones, C. N.: Populism, The Mainstream Theatre, and the Plays of Willy Russell. UMI Dissertation Information Services. Ann Arbor, Michigan 1989, pp. 321–322)

Can you understand why Frank finds Rita refreshing? Imagine what the other students are like.

Does Frank reject the kind of pulp fiction that Rita enjoys?

1. Working class culture

List the points which Rita makes in scene 4 about working class culture and explain them in your own words. Does Frank share Rita's views? What do you think Russell is saying about middle class concepts of the working class?
Why do you think Rita hates politics?

2. 'Only connect'

Rita's description of working class life shows that she now understands Forster's phrase 'only connect'. Now she sees that single aspects of working class life form a whole system. Explain how this system is a vicious circle by filling in this diagram.

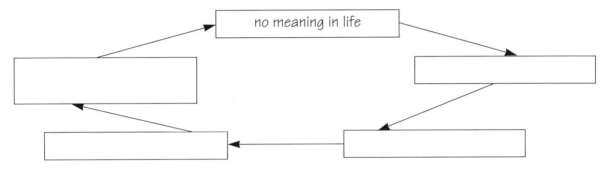

How does Rita try to escape from this vicious circle?

3. Newspapers and social class

Describe how these various British papers present the news. The two articles about the election refer to the 1997 general election in which former Conservative Prime Minister John Major was successfully challenged by Labour's Tony Blair.
Which of these papers are probably of the type Rita mentions?

ELECTION COUNTDOWN

Blair goes straight for prime target

Labour's election bandwagon made its first stop yesterday in the party's most crucial campaign target – the Gloucester seat which the party must win if Tony Blair is to become prime minister.

May 1 **Countdown to the Election**

MAGGIE WEIGHS IN FOR MAJOR

Ex-PM's last-ditch bid to save Tories

By Pascoe Watson
Lady Thatcher mounted a last-ditch bid yesterday to keep alive Tory hopes of a record fifth term.

Only hours after John Major announced at Downing Street that the General Election would be on May 1, she threw her weight behind his campaign.

The ex-Premier warned: "I hear peopl saying it is time for a change. That absurd. If you have got a good builder, dare I say it a good grocer, or a go government, you don't chance. You sti with them and I hope you will stick w us."

Naked Brits' holiday boob

TWENTY British tourists sparked a blazing row with locals when they stripped naked beside shocked families at a Dutch picnic site.

Crash girl found dead by cop dad

By Chris Pharo
A TOP policeman wept yesterday as he told how he found his own daughter dead in a car smash.

4. Choices

Summarise this extract from an article about the mass media and explain how it relates to Rita's feelings about herself and the working class as a whole.

Discuss the suggestion in the first paragraph that people get what they deserve.

When the controllers of the media are not providing a form of covert[1] propaganda for the status quo – and they are not necessarily doing so consciously – they defend what they supply on the ground[2] that they are giving the public what it wants. What happens is that they give the public what they wish it to want, and then interpret acquiescence[3] as approval (...)

Even if the controllers could establish in a particular case that there was a genuine preference for their offering, they would in many cases be found to have created the taste for it. What sells most is rarely the best line, more likely the most strenuously promoted[4], and need bear little or no relation[5] to consumers' wishes. The controllers' measure of success is profit, and they arrange that what is sold is the most profitable (...)

It is the age of the big insult – trivia pays larger dividends[6], therefore trivia must be what is wanted. Is this a deliberate policy to keep the nation cretinized[7] by trivialities or does it stem[8] from a profound belief that the people of this country are cretins[9] from the start?

The cynical view of people is reflected in a no-choice policy, for choice involves some acquaintance with the possibilities, a more than superficial acquaintance. Such a knowledge of the range of things to choose from is just what the controllers in general are unable to supply. The hunt for mass audiences, needed to attract advertising and pay for it, causes the controllers to narrow the field of taste in which people can discriminate: 'they will be kept unaware of what lies beyond the average of experience'.[10]

(Denys Thompson [ed.]: Discrimination and Popular Culture. Penguin 1973, pp. 15–16)

Annotations:
[1] covert – undercover, hidden
[2] on the ground – here: with the reason
[3] acquiescence – apparent acceptance, lack of protest
[4] to promote – here: to advertise
[5] bear ... relation – does not necessarily have anything to do with
[6] pays larger dividents – makes more profit
[7] to cretinize – to make stupid
[8] to stem from – to come from
[9] cretin – stupid person
[10] the average of experience – the norm, what the average person reads, hears and sees

1. Denny's reactions

Look at scenes 4 and 5 and describe Denny's reactions to his wife's studies.
What do you think will happen next?

2. A woman's place is in the home

What do you think the man in the cartoon is saying?
Does the cartoon suggest anything else which Denny might object to?
How does Rita feel about Denny?
Make up a typical argument between Denny and Rita.

Male protests at women improving themselves have a long history. This French cartoon from the 1850s shows a wife, her mind on higher things, pouring boot polish into her husband's drinking chocolate.

3. A metaphor

Russell uses an extended metaphor to explain how important the course is to Rita. Find examples of the images which express this metaphor.

4. Frank, the poet

Why do you think Frank drinks so much? Do you understand what he means by 'Instead of creating poetry I spent – oh – years and years trying to create literature' (p. 41, ll.19/20)?

5. Frank, the cynic

Look at Rita's comments on Frank's character, 'Y' never tell the truth you, do y'?… y' like evade it with jokes an' that' (p. 42, ll.29, 32). How would someone with a better command of the language have expressed this?

1. Macbeth

Explain why Rita wanted to go to the theatre and what she expected. Can you remember feeling like Rita after seeing a certain play or film? How did you feel beforehand? Did you think it would be boring, too?
What does Rita's reaction to Macbeth show about her approach to literature?

2. Tragedy

Look at these headlines. Which ones would Rita describe as 'tragedies'?

1. **BOY, 16, MISSING FOR THREE DAYS**

2. **Six-year-old girl electrocuted by Xmas tree lights**

3. **Couple die in lake trying to save dog**

4. **Tragedy of holiday accident**

5. **Baby saved from fire**

How would you paraphrase what Rita means by 'tragic' events?
Give examples. How does Frank define 'tragedy'?

3. The dinner party

Frank has invited both Rita and Denny to a dinner party at his house. When Rita gets home she tells Denny about it. Imagine their conversation.

Rita: Denny, Frank has invited us both to a dinner party at his house on Saturday night.
Denny: ...

1. Rita's reactions

Imagine you are Rita. You are outside Frank's house and through the window you see his guests, mostly university lecturers. How do you feel? What do you decide to do?

Have you ever felt like this? Do you know or can you imagine someone who might feel like Rita? Imagine you are one of these outsiders and describe your feelings.

2. In the pub

When Rita set off for Frank's dinner party Denny went to the pub with the family. He had to explain why Rita was not with him. Imagine you are Denny. What do you say?

A FRIEND: Where's Rita then?
DENNY   ...

If she were mine...

She should ...

You know what I'd do?

Why don't you ...?

Rita did not go to Frank's. Instead, she went to join her family in the pub. What explanation do you think she gave them?
Was Frank right to invite Rita to dinner or was he naive and thoughtless?

3. In between

Make up a diagram to show which of these people belong in the same groups and which are outsiders: Rita, Frank, Denny, the people in the pub, Rita's mother, Julia, the dinner party guests.

Explain in your own words how Rita feels about her original working class environment and about Frank's middle class, academic one.

4. Rita's decision

When Rita went to the pub she decided she would not go on with her studies. Explain why she changed her mind. What do Rita's and Denny's reactions show about their characters?

What is the dramatic function of Rita's mother?
Do you feel sorry for Denny or pleased because he is happy with life as it is?

5. Why not sing the old song?
Does Frank understand Rita's position? Do you think Russell might be saying something about the class system?

1. Betrayed

How does this cartoon illustrate the conflict between
Rita and Denny?

*"You know what I'd like to
be? A traitor to my class."*

2. Decisions

Work with a partner. One of you describes Rita's situation, the
other Frank's.

— Rita/Frank has to decide whether to/if (s)he wants to...
— If (s)he goes on,...
— ...is (not) sure that/if (s)he wants...
— ...has already made... decision/has not made... decision
   yet.

Does Rita understand Frank's problem? Answer this question by
finishing these sentences.

Frank wants Rita to...
Rita wants Frank to teach her...

How do you think the play will go on? Write your ideas down
on a piece of paper. Then collect them and read them out.

3. Rita goes to her mother's

Rita goes to stay with her mother for a week. Imagine their
conversation when she arrives. Do you think her mother
sympathises with her or is she angry?

1. Summer school

Make a list of the ways in which Rita has changed.
Do you think she is right when she says, 'Frank, you woulda
been dead proud of me?' (p. 55, l.21)?

2. Frank's reactions

Notice how Frank reacts to the 'new' Rita. What is he probably
thinking?

Changes in Rita	Frank's thoughts
– ...	– ...

Comment on Frank's remark, 'I shall be glad to see you go'
(p. 60, l.2). Can you explain the significance of the incident with
the window (p. 58, ll.11 ff.)?

3. Songs of Innocence and Experience

The following text provides some information about Blake's
Songs of Innocence and Experience. Decide why Russell chose
them for Rita to study at summer school.

Blake began writing his two sets of poems, *Songs of Innocence* and *Songs of Experience* in 1789. The first set, *Songs of Innocence*, describes ideals and childlike innocence; the second shows how these ideals turn into illusions in the face of reality. The tone is often bitter. *The Sick Rose* is one of the *Songs of Experience*.

1. Frank's feelings

Prepare some questions which you would like to ask Frank. Find
out, for example, how he feels about:
- Rita being late for her class (scene 2).
- Rita's unnatural voice (scene 2).
- Trish (scene 2).
- how Rita relates to the other students (scene 2).
- Rita's essay (scene 3).
- Rita's remarks on 'boring, insignificant detail' and being
  'trapped' (scene 4).

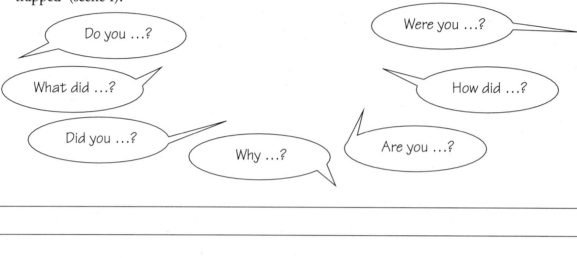

_____

_____

_____

_____

_____

_____

2. Rita's essay

How does Rita feel about Frank's criticism of her essay?
Is Frank right to be disappointed with Rita?

Compare Rita's reaction to the poem with her description of
school in Act I, scene 2 (p. 28, ll. 22–31).
How do you feel about analysing literature? Does it spoil your
pleasure?

3. Frank's downfall

Imagine you were one of the students in Frank's class when he
fell down. Describe what happened to someone who was not
there. How did you feel?
Make up a conversation between Frank just after Frank's
meeting with his superiors.

RITA: ...?
FRANK: ...

4. Reversed roles

Note down evidence from scenes 2–4 which suggests that Frank
and Rita have become more like each other.

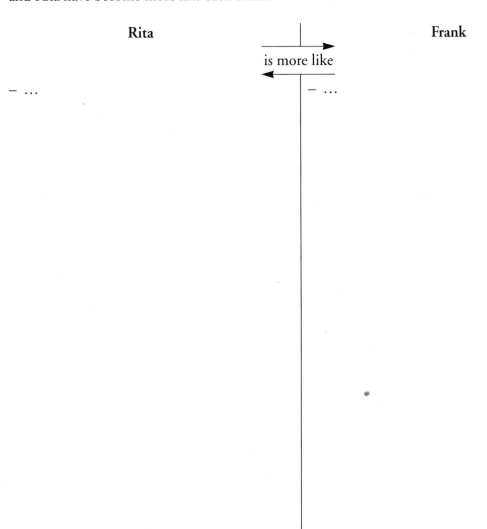

Could Russell be saying something more general about class
barriers by reversing the roles in this way?

5. Frank's poetry

Why did Frank ask Rita for her opinion on his poems?
What is he hoping for?
How do you think their relationship will develop?
How will Rita's life go on?

1. A fine job

Describe Frank's reactions to Rita's opinions. What does he mean by 'I've done a fine job on you' (p. 73, l.4)?
Educating Rita is an autobiographical play. Read this description of Russell's own education. Do you see a parallel with what Frank now dislikes about Rita?

> I came from a house in which we wouldn't have a plant, we wouldn't have a picture, we wouldn't sit at a table, we'd have food on our knees whilst watching telly. So when I first moved into a different world, before I went to college, and started to mix with people, I'd go into people's houses and they'd have all these things – they didn't live their lives for things, it was just a natural expression of their sensibilities on the whole. One used to want not the pictures, not the plants but what one saw as the ritual way of living. A calmer, more fulfilling life. It's only later on that you find out that is just a particular veneer[1] and that life can be just as arid[2], if you think it will be better if you have the right pictures on the wall and the right plants.

Annotations:
[1]veneer – thin layer of wood
[2]arid – dry

(Jones, C.N.: Populism, The Mainstream Theatre, and the Plays of Willy Russell. UMI Dissertation Information Services. Ann Arbor, Michigan 1989, p. 334)

2. The Logical Song

If Frank heard this song he would probably think that it summed up his situation. Can you explain why? What does he dislike about his work and himself? How does he relate to the people around him?

> **Supertramp – THE LOGICAL SONG**
>
> When I was young it seemed that life was so wonderful
> A miracle, oh, it was beautiful, magical
> And all the birds in the trees, well they'd be singing so happily
> Oh, joyfully, oh, playfully watching me
>
> But then they sent me away to teach me how to be sensible
> Logical, oh, responsible, practical
> And they showed me a world where I could be so dependable
> Oh, clinical, oh, intellectual, cynical
>
> There are times when all the world's asleep
> The questions run too deep for such a simple man
> Won't you please, please tell me what we've learned?
> I know it sounds absurd, please tell me who I am
>
> I said, Now watch what you say or they'll be calling you a radical
> A liberal, oh, fanatical, criminal
> Oh won't you sign up your name, we'd like to feel you're acceptable
> Respectable, oh, presentable, a vegetable

© Supertramp, London. Text and music: Rick Davies and Roger Hodgson

3. The quarrel

Imagine you are either Frank or Rita and describe the quarrel to a friend. Explain how you think things will develop.

I had a quarrel with…the other day…

1. Education and Social Class

Pick out a passage from scene 5 in which Russell refers to the
British class system. What is he suggesting?
Do you think Russell is criticising Rita, Frank or both?

In an interview Russell was asked about the class aspect of
his plays.

J. G.	How significant is class in your plays?
W. R.	...So, yes, it is important to me, but increasingly I do see that there are very definite tribes of people in our society and I find that more intriguing. And especially as now it is becoming very confused anyway, because what we are starting to develop in this country, along with some of the countries of Europe, is a very entrenched underclass. It is more and more difficult to talk about any working class. Don't tell me that there is not a working class/middle class divide in this country, because there is... but I don't want to shout about it in my plays. I don't live my life self-consciously worrying on behalf of a deprived, dispossessed class. But the fact is that my sympathies are inevitably with a group of people, a section of society who've drawn the short straw[1]. That's all there is to it. I'm not saying that I like them as people more than I like the people of the middle classes, what I am saying is – these are the people who drew the short straw.
W. R.	... we must have a society in which there really is equal opportunity for all, which is what the 1944 Act[2] was about; equal opportunity, not equality, which it was often mistaken for in the 60s, but we must have a society which allows for all individuals.

(Gill, J.: Willy Russell and His Plays.
Countyvise Ltd. 1996, p. 53 and p. 26)

[1]to draw the short straw-here: to have worse chances than other people
[2]an Act of Parliament which laid the foundation for the modern education system

Check that you have understood Russell's views by ticking the
statements which come closest to his opinions.

1. The British class system is changing. ☐
2. In Britain the class system is disappearing. ☐
3. The working class is turning into the middle class. ☐
4. It is difficult to distinguish between the old working class
   and the new underclass. ☐
5. Russell prefers the working class to the middle class. ☐
6. Russell wants to show that in Britain not everyone has
   the same educational and cultural opportunities. ☐

1. Frank and Rita

What do scene 6 and the stage directions for scene 7 tell us about the relationship between Frank and Rita? Do you think they have been in contact again after their quarrel?

2. Frank, a good teacher?

Rita came back to thank Frank. Explain what he has taught her to enable her to pass exams.
Do you agree with Rita that Frank is a good teacher?
Think about what a good teacher should be like.

3. A change in Rita

Do you see any changes in Rita since the quarrel? Do you like her better now?

4. Trish

Trish's suicide attempt contributed to the change in Rita. Can you explain how?
Think of how Rita described Trish and her other new friends to Frank and draw conclusions about Trish's dramatic function in the play.

5. Rita's future

Put the choices which Rita says she has in this diagram. What else do you think she might do?

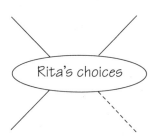

Rita's choices

Write what you think will happen next on a slip of paper, then collect them. Do most of the class agree?

Student Profile

Lynn Blackadder
London
'Although I left school with enough qualifications to go to university, I wasn't interested in full-time studying and wanted to get a job. After working for two years as a secretary in Edinburgh, a colleague who was studying with the Open University told me about the arts courses they offered... Five years later I have found my niche in life: I'm working in London for Britain's leading art charity, the National Art Collections Fund.'

('Courses, Diplomas and BA/BSc Degrees'. The Open University, Milton Keynes 1997)

34

6. The film ending

Compare the ending of the film with that of the play. Which do you prefer?
Suggest reasons why Rita does not want to accompany Frank to Australia.

7. Choices

Does it matter what Rita decides to do?
Do you see any wider social and political implications in Rita's position at the end?

This poem was written by Liz Lochhead. Compare Liz's life with that of her friend, Mary. What was the same? What was different?

Liz Lochhead
The Choosing

We were first equal Mary and I
with the same coloured ribbons in mouse-
coloured hair,
and with equal shyness
we curtseyed to the lady councillor
for copies of Collins' Children's Classics.[1]
First equal, equally proud.

Best friends too Mary and I
a common bond in being cleverest (equal)
in our small school's small class.
I remember
the competition for top desk
or to read aloud the lesson
at school service.
And my terrible fear
of her superiority at sums.

I remember the housing scheme[2]
where we both stayed.
The same house, different homes,
where the choices were made.

I don't know exactly why they moved,
but anyway they went.
Something about a three-apartment
and a cheaper rent.
But from the top deck of the high-school bus

I'd glimpse among the others on the corner
Mary's father, mufflered, contrasting strangely
with the elegant greyhounds by his side.

He didn't believe in high-school education,
especially for girls,
or in forking out[3] for uniforms.

Ten years later on a Saturday –
I am coming home from the library –
sitting near me on the bus,
Mary
with a husband who is tall,
curly haired, has eyes
for no one else but Mary.
Her arms are round the full-shaped vase
that is her body.
Oh, you can see where the attraction lies
in Mary's life –
not that I envy her, really.

And I am coming from the library
with my arms full of books.
I think of the prizes that were ours for the taking
and wonder when the choices got made
we don't remember making.

(Liz Lochhead, Dreaming Frankenstein and Other Poems. Polygon 1984.)

[1] Collin's Children's Classics – Liz and Mary were both the best pupils at school. They shared the prize, the book 'Children's Classics', published by Collins. It was given to them by a local politician, a lady councillor.

[2] housing scheme – a housing estate where all the houses are the same

[3] to fork out (sl.) – to spend money

8. Liz and Rita

Pick out the lines which show that the poem has the same main idea as *Educating Rita*. Support your answer by quoting from the last scene of the play.

9. A press conference

Imagine you are journalists and are going to hold a press conference with Willy Russell about his play. (He also wrote the screenplay for the film.) In groups write down your questions. Then decide on one person to play Russell and interview him or her.

Willy Russell

10. Your feelings

Where would you put the play or the film on this scale?

hot	I thought it was really good because …
warm	It was quite good, but I couldn't get really interested in it. I …
cold	It didn't really interest me very much because …

angry – sad – upset – upsetting – happy
emotional – exciting – boring – bored –
depressed – depressing – interested –
interesting – surprised – surprising –
pleased – amused – amusing – funny – disappointed –
disappointing – poignant – touching – …

Did the story make you think about anything? Did it say anything to you about your own life or your own way of thinking?

11. Designing a programme or advertisement

Collect some theatre programmes and advertisements for films, then design one for *Educating Rita*. Look for magazine pictures, draw your own, or take some photos to illustrate the most important scenes.

Write a short summary of the story and make up a cast list from your classmates.

Rita – a modern day Eliza?

As you see from these reviews, *Educating Rita* has often been
described as a modern *Pygmalion*.

LIKE Roots and Pygmalion. Willy
Russell's Educating Rita is one of
those plays in which a female pupil
learns from and eventually outstrips
her male teacher. It suffers initially
from a harvest of Liverpudlian corn
but it grows into a touching and quite
complex play about the melancholic
way education often pulls people apart
instead of bringing them together...
Julie Walters who graduates from a
chipper perkiness to a real self-
awareness: an Eliza who would out-
argue her Higgins rather than ever
return to him.

Guardian, Michael Billington,
17/6/80

By ERIC SHORTER
WITH ITS echoes of "Pygmalion"
and "The Corn is Green", Willy
Russell's new play "Educating Rita"
seems underdramatised and fitter per-

Daily Telegraph, 18/6/80

TREADING eagerly in the
upwardly mobile footsteps
of Shaw's Eliza Doolittle,
and Arnold Wesker's
Beatie Bryant comes the
heroine of Willy Russell's
Educating Rita (Ware-
house), whose real name is
Susan.

Observer, 22/6/80

A WARMLY written two-hander,
Educating Rita (Warehouse),
follows the well-worn route which
leads from the humdrum everyday
world to the tutor's study – an Open
Sesame to a better life for an aspiring
young girl. Like Eliza Doolittle, this
particular applicant is spirited, lively
and soon in charge of the situation.

Sunday Telegraph, 22/6/80

In groups, note down some similarities and differences between
the two plays without putting them into any kind of order. Then
put your ideas into this table.

ELIZA AND RITA	Similarities	Differences
Social class		
Motives		
Personalities		
How they change		

HIGGINS AND FRANK	Similarities	Differences
Attitude to pupils		
Changes in relationship with pupils		
Structure of plot		
Themes/Authors' intentions		

Exchange your list with other groups until you arrive at one the whole class agrees on.

A1
First impressions

Because the language is very difficult it is advisable to read the play in relatively small sections, especially at the beginning. It is not essential to understand every word and all the allusions, only the general idea.

1. The story
Working in groups or pairs, students try to put the quotations into some sort of order. Alternatively, groups can be given slips of paper with a quotation on each and asked to work out what the play might be about. They can speculate as to what sort of people Frank and Rita are (age, social class, interests, educational background etc.).

● Answer
1-11-8-2-14-3-9-4-13-5-10-6-12-7.

What else would you …?

Suggested questions:
Who is the teacher? How old is Rita? Is she a youngish pupil or an older student? Where does the story take place? etc.

A2
Act 1, scene 1: Open university; the author

1. The beginning – Starting with the video
Video: Students watch the first scene of the video up to where Frank takes the bottle of whisky from his shelf.

● Answer
University lecturer, probably in England (Victorian buildings, traditional setting), unhappy, frustrated (needs whisky).

The scenes are shown again and students check their impressions. They then read the first scene up to p. 10, 1.8 (Frank: … erotic). It is not necessary for the learners to understand every detail, they should just get the general idea.

2. First impressions: Frank
A detailed study of the phone conversation on p. 8 helps students to compile their first impressions of Frank.
Working in pairs or groups the learners fill in the table. (See below.)

In pairs students try to make up the whole conversation. If they find it difficult they could split it into two halves, working down as far as *Woman: Then why did you take it on?* and then exchanging roles.

● Answer
The woman's part could be reconstructed as follows:

Frank: Yes?
Woman: Are you still there?
Frank: Of course …
Woman: Why?
Frank: Because …
Woman: Oh no.
Frank: Tch.
Woman: You didn't tell me.
Frank: Of course …
Woman: But I've prepared dinner.
Frank: But darling …
Woman: Will you go to the pub afterwards?
Frank: Yes …

Woman: Then why did you take it on?
Frank: Oh God, why …
Woman: For the money.
Frank: Yes.
Woman: To pay for the drink.
Frank: Yes I suppose …

Quotation	Conclusions
– He manages … receiver	– alcoholic
– I've got … coming	– lecturer, teaches for O.U.; impatient, bad-tempered
– you shouldn't … late. Look … guilt in me	– relationship with woman not harmonious; she probably does not like his drinking
– Oh God … drink	– only agreed to teach course because needed extra money for drink.
– I like my lamb … burn; I don't need determination …	– witty

Woman: Oh Frank!/But Frank…
Frank: Oh, for God's sake…
Woman: What shall I do about the dinner?
Frank: Yes, well…
Woman: I can't. It'll get burnt/be spoiled.
Frank: Look…
Woman: How can I leave it in the oven?
Frank: Because…
Woman: Of course it can.
Frank: Darling…
Woman: Are you determined to go to the pub?
Frank: What…

3. Rita

Video: Students are shown Rita's arrival at university up to the point where she walks up the stairs towards Frank's room. They should realise that she does not look like a normal student and that this is the first time she has been there. They speculate as to why she is there.

Do you think…?

● Answer
Rita is probably not a normal student. She does not look like one. She does not know where to go and has to ask for directions. Maybe she is a new secretary. Perhaps she is related to one of the students etc.

Does this information…?
With the help of the information about the Open University students can explain Rita's probable appearance at the university.

● Answer
Rita is probably a new Open University student.

Read the extracts…

● Answer
– *There are no entry qualifications for the Open University (except for higher degrees).*
– *You don't need to take time off work (75% of the students remain in full-time employment throughout their studies).*
– *The OU is for people over 18 who are normally resident in the UK or elsewhere in the European Union.*
– *Students are attached to a tutor and are expected to produce regular written work. In many cases there is also an end of course examination.*

If the woman…

● Answer
From the woman's general appearance students might draw the conclusion that she is not a particularly intellectual type. She might, for instance, be some sort of secretary who needs to learn about computing for her job. She may have been sent on the course by her employers. The lecturer is probably her tutor.

Additional information:

This additional information about the OU gives further clues about the woman's background.

The Open University
The Labour Party first broached the idea of the Open University in the 1960s. It would be an educational service, or 'university of the air', which employed television, radio, and correspondence courses. It was intended to give educational opportunities (or a 'second chance') to people who had not been able to proceed to further and higher education[1]. It was particularly hoped that the courses might appeal to working-class students who had left school at the official school-leaving age, and who now wished to broaden their horizons.

The Open University opened in 1969, and its first courses started in 1971. By the mid-eighties, there were some 70,000 students at one stage or another of their long, part-time courses. About 7,000 students of all ages and from very different walks of life receive degrees from the Open University each year.

Dedication, stamina, and perseverance are necessary to complete the Open University programmes. Students do not attend any one institution, but receive their lessons and lectures at home, partly by correspondence courses and partly by special television (BBC2) and radio broadcasts. Part-time tutors in local areas mark the students' written work, and meet the students regularly to discuss their progress. There are also special weekend and other courses throughout the year, which are held at universities, polytechnics, and colleges.

[1] further education – colleges for 16–18-year-olds, e.g. technical colleges; higher education – universities, from 18 onwards

(Oakland, John: British Civilization. Routledge, London 1989, pp. 166–167)

It can be concluded that the woman is probably from the working-class and left school at the official school-leaving age. She did not proceed to further and higher education. But now she wishes to broaden her horizons. Since the woman is older than the average student she probably has a job and has enrolled as a part-time student. She may even have had a child and then decided to go on with her education.

4. Rita's entrance

Video: The students watch the scene in which Rita enters Frank's study, up to the point where she goes to look at the picture. As they watch they make notes on Rita's personality, probable background and on Frank's reactions.

Working in groups or with a partner and referring to the text for help (p. 9), the students make up a more conventional entrance. Normally, Rita would introduce herself by name, but we do not yet know her surname. The students' suggestions will vary.

Suggestion
Frank: *Come in! Come in!*
Rita: *Hello. I'm the new student on the Open University course. I made an appointment with you/You wanted to see me.*
Frank: *Oh yes. Come in. Sit down, please.*
Rita: *Thank you.*

How does Frank react…?

● Answer
Frank is 'slightly confused'. He would have expected her to come in more quietly, to introduce herself and to generally show him more respect. Normally a new student would not begin by criticising his door handle. She would probably not swear either.

What conclusions…?
Rita is a very open, direct, spontaneous person. She is obviously not very well educated. The way she comes into the room suggests that she is not used to formal situations and does not know how to behave appropriately. She does not realise, either, that Frank's question 'You are…?' is a common formula when asking someone to introduce themselves.

5. 'Normal' universities

Compare…

● Answer (see table below)

6. A new student

As students fill in the gapped interview they will probably realize that the student is Russell himself.

INTERVIEWER: When were you born and where?
STUDENT: In 1947, in Whiston, just outside Liverpool.

INTERVIEWER: How old were you when you left school?
STUDENT: Fifteen.
INTERVIEWER: What kind of school did you go to?
STUDENT: Secondary school.
INTERVIEWER: Did you work hard at school?
STUDENT: No, not at all. I wasn't interested, you see. The only thing I enjoyed was the reading lessons. That's when I first started thinking I might become a writer myself.
INTERVIEWER: What did you do when you left school?
STUDENT: Well, there were lots of discussions, even rows, about what I should do. And eventually my mother said I should become a ladies' hairdresser. So I did.
INTERVIEWER: How long did you do it for/work as a hairdresser?
STUDENT: Six years. When we weren't too busy I read. But eventually I decided that if I was really going to become a writer I would have to do something about it.
INTERVIEWER: So what did you do?
STUDENT: Well, I realized that I needed to be with the kind of people who would understand, that I would have to move into the academic world.
INTERVIEWER: Was that an easy decision?
STUDENT: No, it wasn't an easy one. Because I had to leave the kind of people, the kind of environment I had grown up in. I knew people wouldn't understand, that they'd be hurt.
INTERVIEWER: So what did you do you?
STUDENT: I decided to become a student. That way I would be able to learn a job. And I'd have time to do some writing.
INTERVIEWER: But you didn't have the qualifications to get here, did you?
STUDENT: No, I didn't. And I couldn't go to night school to get them because it would have taken too long. I had to find a full-time course. But first I had to earn the money to pay for it.
INTERVIEWER: And how did you do that?
STUDENT: I took a night-shift job in a factory, cleaning oil from the girders high above the machinery. It was very dangerous, but the money was good. As soon as I had enough I stopped and enrolled here as a student.

	Rita	Frank
'normal' university	*a proper university, the ordinary university, the real students*	
The Open University	*degrees for dishwashers*	*It's supposed to embrace a more comprehensive studentship*

41

Can you guess...?

● Answer
– *Willy Russell*

Additional information: Willy Russell

Russell grew up in a working class family on a housing estate just outside Liverpool. His father worked in a factory before he bought a fish-and-chip shop and his mother had a job in a warehouse. Like most of the other youngsters on the estate he, too, had the antipathy towards education common to his environment and social class. He left school at 15 with only one O-level, in English, and the vague idea that he wanted to become a writer. However, with his social background he had no idea how to go about it.

Yet, although he regarded art as something outside his sphere, he became interested in the Liverpool Beat Poets (among them the Roger McGough mentioned by Rita in Act 1, scene 1) and in folk-music, playing the guitar in pubs. Russell describes his initial distaste for plays and the theatre as follows, "Theatre had always seemed to me a highbrow slap in the face to people like me. I just couldn't relate to it, either culturally or socially; it didn't seem to me to be about people like me, and people like me never seemed to go and look at it." (*The Independent*: Profile, 23/1/88). But this all changed when his girlfriend, now his wife, took him to Liverpool's Everyman Theatre. The early seventies was an important period for regional drama and new, local talent was being encouraged. Russell said, "They turned it into a real local people's theatre... The working class voice was allowed to be heard" (*The Independent*, 23/1/88). This experience showed him what kind of things he wanted to write. It also made him decide to study drama at a teacher's training college, St Katherine's College of Education. But first he had to take his O-level and A-level exams. Then he needed to raise the money to pay for his studies (details in the interview, A2, exercise 6). His reasons for returning to full-time education were the same as Rita's: he 'wanted to know everything' and, most importantly, wanted to have more control over his own life, to choose how to live it. Success came relatively quickly. One of his first plays was spotted at the Edinburgh Festival and he was asked to write a play for the Everyman Theatre. He wrote *John, Paul, George, Ringo and Bert*, about his experiences as a 14-year-old Beatles fan. At the time Russell had a teaching job, but the popularity of his play enabled him to give it up and become a full-time writer.

Russell is one of a group of left-wing Merseyside writers which has recently emerged. It includes Alan Bleasdale, the playwright (*Boys from the Blackstuff*), Phil Redmond, the writer-producer (*Brookside, Grange Hill*) and Frank Clarke, the writer (*Letter to Brezhnev*). They have been immensely popular in the theatre, television and film.

Almost every theatre in Britain has staged Russell's *Educating Rita*, his most autobiographical play and also the one which gave him his international reputation. He was closely involved in making the film version. Almost equally popular is his more recent *Shirley Valentine*. Yet, despite his fame, Russell has remained in Liverpool, refusing to move to London partly out of fear that he would be sucked into the middle classes.

Homework
Students read on up to p. 13.

A 3
Act 1, scene 1: highbrow/lowbrow culture; social class

1. 'Good' poetry
Russell is obviously using Rita as a mouthpiece for his own ideas. Students will probably understand Rita's comment and may even share her views on the elitism often associated with 'good' literature (or music).

● Answer
Rita's comment could be seen as an attack on the esoteric nature of literary criticism. It suggests that literary critics set up artificial standards of good and bad in order to establish a literary elite.
a) *They love literature for its own sake.*
b) *They see literature as a means of gaining* ☐
   social prestige.
c) *They will read any kind of literature.* ☑
d) *They prefer literature which is difficult to* ☐
   understand.
e) *They think that if they classify literature which* ☑
   is difficult to understand as 'good', they will
   seem clever. ☑

2. Tell me what you watch and I'll tell you who you are

Students should understand the difference between the German and English meanings of 'programme': a TV programme – eine einzige Fernsehsendung/alle Sendungen an einem Tage/eine Fernsehprogramm-zeitschrift.

● Answer
Rita's remarks suggest that the working class tend to prefer entertainment which is relatively easy to understand ('lowbrow' entertainment), whereas educated middle class people like Frank would prefer something more 'highbrow'. Students might circle the following programmes:

People from Rita's background: any of BBC 1's or BBC 2's programmes except the 'Open University' (BBC 2, 12.30) and the ITV film.
People like Frank: BBC 2's 'The Goldring…', 'A Tale…'; ITV's 'A Lesson…', 'The Money…'; Channel 4.

3. Rita's environment

● Answer
p. 13: these stuck-up idiots I meet… It's not their fault; they can't help it. But sometimes I hate them.
Rita feels that the people she lives among have very limited, narrow lives. They cling on to what they know and automatically reject anything new, without even trying to understand it. Sometimes she hates them for this because they also prevent her from breaking out and doing new things. But she understands that it is not their fault. She realises that their behaviour has something to do with their poor education.

If you were…
Students might suggest a picture showing someone crying out for help, as in Edvard Munch's "The Scream". Or they might see Rita as someone trying to escape from somewhere, in a cage or a prison cell.

4. Rita's needs

● Answer
Rita wants to know about the kind of literature and art which she does not normally come into contact with. It is the kind of art which working class people normally reject as 'posh' or 'highbrow' and which they associate with the middle class. They tend to reject it automatically, without even trying to understand it. Rita, however, wants to be more in control of her own life. She feels she can only decide what she likes or dislikes if she understands it properly first.
By 'freedom' she means the freedom from having to behave in a certain way because of a lack of knowledge and understanding. If she had a better education she

would not, for instance, reject certain TV programmes simply because she thought they were 'highbrow'. 'She would be able to understand them and could still choose whether to watch them or not. She would also have the freedom to choose whether to swear or not. Russell himself answered the question of what the OU course means to Rita in an interview (Glaap, in: Educating Rita. Diesterweg, 1981, p. 95). 'She does want to be able to sit down and discuss books and art and music and to be spiritually fed and, to stay in the metaphor, she feels that she's starving in her present social stratum, that it's arid and that if she moves in this other stratum it will be some sort of oasis.'
Russell then draws a parallel to his own life. He goes on: 'This was certainly something I felt before I went back to education. I overvalued to a ludicrous extent the idea of education, what, you know, college and higher education was and went through a period being very much like Rita.'

How do you think…?
Students will probably suggest that Rita's family and friends will have no understanding whatsoever for her decision to study. There will probably be a lot of difficulties and arguments.

Does 'freedom' …?
Students write down a few words which they associate with the word 'freedom' and discuss their ideas.

5. Highbrow and lowbrow literature

The insight that the British working and middle classes are divided along cultural lines (the kind of television programmes they watch) is widened to include the type of literature which they prefer. A link can be made with the changes in Russell's own literary preferences, expressed in the text in A3, 1. Students should be made familiar with the terms high/highbrow and low/lowbrow.

● Answer
Frank: T. S. Eliot, Dickens, Henry James, Dylan Thomas, E. M. Forster, Yeats, Oscar Wilde.
Rita: Roger McGough, Rita Mae Brown, Frank Harris, (T. S. Eliot, slightly)

Students can try to find out from histories of literature what sort of works these authors produced. The main insight should be that the ones Frank knows are regarded as writers of great quality.

Do you think…?
Rita would not be able to pass an exam on English literature yet because she does not know enough about it. She cannot tell the difference between good quality literature and popular pulp fiction. Also, she does not

know how to analyse literature. She has to learn the methods. Her approach is completely subjective.

Quite a few humorous misunderstandings arise between Rita and Frank because of their different levels of knowledge and education: Yeats, the poet (pronounced like Yates) – Yates, the wine shop, Eliot, the poet – Elliot Ness, the Chicago policeman who caught the gangster, Al Capone.

Homework

Students read on to the end of the scene and do exercise 5.

A4
Act I, scene 1: culture, language and social class

1. Elite culture, popular culture

● Answer

Rita is more conscious of the class differences between them. She is altogether more aware of social class.
– p. 17, l.11/12 f.: Rita suggests that Frank prefers the supposedly more intellectual BBC television channel.
– p. 17, l.15 ff.: Rita supposes that Frank is educated enough to know which type of food is healthy, such as the low-cholestorol 'Flora' margarine instead of butter and whole wheat, brown bread rather than the normal white. (Houses which have a pebble-dashed facade look rough and uneven because pebbles have been mixed in with the concrete). Rita is implying that Frank is a 'muesli-freak'.

Using… (see table below)

Compare the tastes…
Students will have no difficulty in seeing that people like Rita tend to prefer popular culture, whereas the more educated, like Frank, have more elitist tastes.

2. There's 'talking' and 'talkin'

● Answer

Some of the points in the extract are true of Rita's speech: her grammar is simpler than Frank's, her sentences are often unfinished and her vocabulary is not as extensive as Frank's.

What important conclusion…
These differences in speech codes are important with regards to the educational system. Most schools are dominated by middle-class teachers who use the "formal" or "elaborated" speech code. This means that the working-class child has the additional difficulty of having to learn new speech patterns.

If you were…
Students try to suggest ways of improving the chances of working class children, possibly by changing the curriculum to include material which is closer to their own speech and mentality. The following quotation shows how Russell himself feels about the problem and how he tries to improve the situation.

Russell has strong views on the working classes' attempts to gain access to middle-class culture.: "Whilst the working-classes are accused of being philistines, there is a general attempt in this country to withhold culture from them … Literature is an invention by the middle-classes for their own benefit. The working-classes haven't accepted literacy yet, which is why it is so difficult teaching working-class kids whose traditions are in the spoken word. That's why I write for the theatre, because it's connected with the spoken rather than the written word."

Note, too, the following comment on Russell's plays:

"What sustains and characterises his best work is a raging, bitter sense of injustice."

(Both quotations from: Charles, Timothy: The First Ten Years. In: *Drama*. 2nd Quarter 1083, No. 148. Published by The British Theatre Association.)

Elite culture	Popular culture
– opera – ballet – "serious" poetry and novels/classic novels – "serious" music, e.g. symphonies	– comic strips – most TV programs and radio shows – romances, detective and science fiction novels – popular music, e.g. rock, rap, country-western – fashions, fads, sports – situation comedies (sit-coms) – action-adventure shows

Fill in this table...

	Frank	Rita
Type of sentences	– longer, more complicated	– short, jerky
Hesitation (fillers)	– no hesitation, no 'fillers'	– hesitation: 'fillers' 'y'know, like'
Repetition	– no repetition	– 'dead, take the piss'
Pronunciation	– precise, clear	– sloppy: 'an', wanna'
Vocabulary	– 'absolutely serious' (more sophisticated) – more varied and sophisticated	– 'dead serious' (colloquial, slangy, bad language 'take the piss' (make jokes, take the mickey out of s.o. or sth.)

3. 'Translating' Rita's speech
Rephrasing Rita's words should help the students to feel of the difference in the two language codes.

● Answer
I'm very/absolutely/extremely serious. Look, I know I often joke about things/it might seem as if I'm not serious, but I really mean what I say. I turn things into jokes because I'm not very confident, although I really want to be.

4. Frank, an acceptable teacher?

● Answer
Rita admits that she used bad language to 'test' Frank. She probably expected a 'respectable', rather stiff academic. She likes Frank because he accepts and respects her for what she is.
- *If Frank had objected to Rita's swearing she would have left.*
- *Rita can only accept a teacher who accepts her way of speaking, even if his own code is different.*
Students will probably understand Rita's feelings and may even be able to give example of their own – the feeling of rejection when their use of language is regarded as inferior (vocabulary, accent).

5. Out of step
The term 'out of step' is taken from dancing. It is as if someone is dancing to a different tune or rhythm to everyone else.

● Answer
- *Rita feels that she cannot talk to her family. Although she normally talks a lot, at home she does not say much. She enjoys talking to Frank because she feels he is closer to her intellectually than her family (p. 14, ll.5–7).*
- *Rita does not want to do the expected thing and have a baby (pp. 18–19). Neither her husband nor the*

neighbours, the people 'round our way' would understand her desire to discover herself first.
- *When Rita tries to explain to her husband that she wants a better life her husband can only think in material terms and suggests buying a house in a different area (p. 19, ll.1 ff.).*
- *Rita also feels different from her customers, 'these stuck-up idiots... sometimes I hate them' (p. 13, l.6).*

How do Rita's comments...?
Rita criticises her customers for thinking that changing their hairstyles will make them into new people. Her own action of taking the university course is the beginning of a change in herself. She realises that real change involves the whole personality: 'if you want to change y' have to do it from the inside, don't y'? Know (Y'know) like I'm doin' (p. 17, ll.25–27).

What... name?
Rita's changing her name contradicts her belief that any change has to come from within and involve the whole of the personality. Like her customers' changes of hairstyle, it is only a superficial change. However, it is a first step towards becoming a different person, or rather to discovering the potential she feels she has.
Students may suggest that her choice of name is not particularly suitable, since Rita Mae Brown is not famous for producing 'good' literature.

6. Rita and Frank – a paradox
Each student writes one of the sentences on a slip of paper and completes it. This exercise is also preparation for the more extensive written task which follows.

Suggestions
Rita: *My life is boring/empty/sterile/...I feel frustrated/unhappy... To me, Frank represents education/freedom/life/...*

Frank: My life is boring/empty/sterile/…I feel frustrated/unhappy… To me, Rita represents a breath of fresh air/life…

Students then take it in turns to read out what they have written, so that 'Rita' and 'Frank' speak alternately.

Can you see a paradox?
Both Rita and Frank are unhappy and frustrated with their lives. Paradoxically both try to escape to each other's worlds. Rita sees in Frank the key to a better, freer life. Frank sees in her the freshness and liveliness which he finds missing "I think…air…in this room for years" (p. 18, l.8).

7. A breath of fresh air

For some reason Frank did not want to teach the Open University course at all. But when he meets Rita he sees just how wrong he was to agree to it (p. 20). Rita expects much more than his other students and he is afraid he will not be able to satisfy her demands. He knows how much the course means to her and does not want this responsibility. Frank finds Rita a refreshing change from his other students because she is more spontaneous and enthusiastic. Because she knows nothing about literary analysis she constantly asks him to explain and justify things that the other students would normally take for granted.

Students can be given help in the form of vocabulary aids, or even a gap text for less able students. For example:
- The first surprise was / doesn't work / swore at it / get it fixed
- The next thing was / erotic
- asked me / for the money
- absolutely no idea about / liked it so much / changed her name
- learn everything / 'discover herself' / frustrated / something better
- intelligent / enthusiastic / hungry for / honest / doesn't like something / says so / mind untrained / subjective, emotional terms
- want to take her on / expects so much / huge responsibility / lose spontaneity / honesty / become just like the others / parroting / so-called 'experts'

● Answer
"Do you know, a breath of fresh air came into my room today for the first time in years. You see, I've taken on an Open University course and a young woman came to see me today, a hairdresser. The first surprise was the way she came into the room. The handle doesn't work properly and she swore at it. Then she told me I should get it fixed. The next thing was that she noticed a picture and said it was very erotic! I wasn't sure how to react to her. I don't really think I liked her very much. Then she asked me if I had taken the course on for the money – I had, of course. But, do you know, she has absolutely no idea about literature. When I mentioned Yeats she thought I meant Yates' wine lodge! She once read a book by Rita Mae Brown and liked it so much she changed her name to Rita. She's really very funny. She made me laugh and gradually I started to like her. I began to listen to her.
She says she wants to learn everything, wants to 'discover herself'. She's frustrated with her way of life and wants something better. She's very intelligent and very enthusiastic – hungry for education really. She's also very honest – if she doesn't like something she says so. But her mind is untrained. She only thinks in subjective, emotional terms.
I don't really want to take her on. She expects so much, it's a huge responsibility. And I don't want her to lose her honesty and spontaneity. It would be awful if she became just like the other students, parroting the opinions of so-called 'experts'. I told her to find a different tutor, but she insists on coming to me. I'm not sure how the whole thing will develop.

Homework
Students read scene 2.

A 5
Act I, scene 2: public schools

1. Public schools
Working in groups students pick out the relevant details.

● Answer
Croft House: individual care and guidance, friendly family community, help each girl to achieve her full potential, stables, riding school, wide variety of extra curricular and weekend activities;
Cheltenham College: caring environment, parkland setting, superb facilities;
Kingham Hill: small classes allowing for individual attention, small, family run.

Students may note that Croft House and Cheltenham College both mention airports. The conclusion can be drawn that many pupils come from wealthy families who either live or work abroad and who can afford frequent air trips.
The article 'Kitted out for Eton' refers to Prince Charles' eldest son William's entrance to Eton. It gives an idea how much uniforms cost. This, beside the fees, would have prevented Rita from attending a public school. Fees are mentioned in the extract from the 'Christian Science Monitor'. Some places

are free for the less well-off and there are scholarships, but it is really only the wealthy who can afford a public school education. Parents send their offspring to public schools for a variety of reasons. With some it is a family tradition, others are attracted by their high academic reputations, their social prestige and the guaranteed entrance into the top levels of society. Also, they offer a quiet, protected atmosphere with their large, peaceful grounds and atmosphere of learning.

There is an excellent, very poignant film about two working class parents who make huge sacrifices in order to send their daughter to a public school, *A Class Act* (VCI Distribution Ltd., 36 Caxton Way, Watford, Herts WD1 8UF). The daughter gradually moves up the social ladder and becomes integrated. Simultaneously, however, she grows away from her parents and even despises them. Nevertheless, the parents are delighted that their daughter has managed to climb the social ladder.

Additional information:

British schools
State schools: free, mostly comprehensives, a few grammar schools.
Public schools
- About 7% of British pupils attend public schools, also known as private or independent schools.
- Public schools charge fees, but also offer scholarships and free places for pupils from less well-off families. The pupils are mostly from upper and upper middle class families.
- Pupils and teachers live at school (boarding schools) and only go home for the holidays.
- Most public schools are for boys, but recently some have begun to accept girls.
- Public schools have high academic standards and small classes. Additional help can be provided for weaker students.
- Emphasis is placed on character training (good manners, sense of responsibility); the schools train their pupils for positions of leadership.
- The most famous public schools: Westminster and Winchester, both founded in 1382, Eton (1440), Rugby (1557) and Harrow (1571).
- Although only 7% of British pupils attend public schools, a disproportionate number of them (over half of all the entrants) go on to the top universities, Oxford and Cambridge (Oxbridge). The schools fulfil an important role in British society, because their students

become the elite of the next generation. Power still lies in the hands of this 'Oxbridge' elite. Public school pupils have traditionally been preferred for high status professions: politics, business, the professions (law, medicine, higher education), the higher ranks of the civil service and the armed services. Just as important are the contacts, the 'old boy' network. According to a survey by the 'Economist' magazine[1] two-thirds of those with top jobs in government, industry, finance and the arts have had a private education and over half went to Oxbridge.

[1] Quoted in: The Guardian, 19. 12. 1992: "Oxbridge generation still finds room at the top."

2. Frank and public schools

● Answer
Frank probably dislikes the elitism of public schools.

Would you…?
The discussion of whether students would have liked to go to a public school or not should consider the following aspects: scholarly atmosphere, good academic standards, propects of good jobs, contacts with the social elite, learning to be independent, living away from home, the expense.

A 6
Act I, scene 2: Rita's school days; literary analysis

1. Rita's school days
The article is about a special school for very intelligent children and shows that, even there, pupils exert tremendous pressure on each other to conform.

● Answer
p. 23, ll. 25 – 28: But studyin'… not allowed

How would Rita…?
The task can be done in groups or with a partner. Vocabulary from the article is useful for the first task.
a) *If I had worked hard at school I would have been rejected by my peers/the others/I would have been an outsider/they would have pushed me out.*
b) *Where I lived you were not allowed to change/be different.*
c) *All my friends expected me to be interested in music, clothes and boys.*
d) *They did not expect me to work hard at school/be interested in school.*

Additional information:

> The value of education for personal development is a thread which runs through Russell's work. Most of his plays are about people trying to escape from the culture they were born into. Rita is aware that she will have to pay a high price for opting out of her environment, but is convinced that her new life will be more meaningful.
>
> Russell is bitter about the fact that the working class have been deprived of a good education and the chance to participate more fully in culture. He feels that they have not been offered the opportunities to make choices about the kinds of lives they would like to lead.

> millions of new houses there and flats, and everyone said there were gangs with bike chains and broken bottles and truck spanners. What everyone said was right; playtime had nothing to do with play, it was about survival. Thugs roamed the concrete and casually destroyed anything that couldn't move fast enough. Dinner time was the same only four times as long.
>
> If you were lucky enough to survive the food itself then you had to get out into the playground world of protection rackets, tobacco hustlers, trainee contract killers and plain no-nonsense sadists. And that's without the teachers!"

(Educating Rita. Diesterweg, pp. 89–90).

2. Girls and school

● Answer

Song:
Girls from Rita's background were probably not expected to get a good education. They were expected to marry, have children and stay at home. In scene 1 Rita told Frank that she felt 'out of step' because she did not fit in with the traditional image of women from her social class (p. 18, ll.20 ff.). Her husband wants a child and the others 'round our way' would not understand her desire to 'discover' herself.

Like Rita, the girl in the song wanted to break the traditional image, and be an engineer. But the people around her would not allow her to break away. Instead, she had to learn the traditional female skill of typing ('typing... sure to need') until the time when she had a baby.

Additional information:

> Russell himself did not enjoy school much. In an interview he once described his school experiences. Students will recognise the similarities to the passage on pp. 23–24,
>
> "When I was eleven they sent me to a secondary school in Huyton. Like all the other Knowsley kids I was frightened of Huyton. There were

3. School and real life

● Answer

From Rita's comments it can be deduced that her associations would be as follows:
REAL LIFE: *direct, first-hand experience, fun, enjoyment, enthusiasm;*
SCHOOL: *second-hand experience, discussions, descriptions, writing, analysing.*

Look at Frank's...
Frank's comment suggests that he feels education excludes real life. He thinks that education can spoil enjoyment by making people analyse things too much. Interest can be destroyed if it is turned into tasks, essays and reports. Eventually, pupils will be afraid to show any interest in anything.
Students can discuss this point of view and make suggestions for improving the situation.

4. Analysing literature

In groups or with a partner students use the vocabulary in the centre of the table to contrast Frank's and Rita's approaches to literature.

● Answer

Frank	Rita
Students of literature should be objective/write objective criticisms/approach literature almost as a science/support their opinions by referring to established literary critics/never be subjective	Literature should be about real life and its problems
Literature need not be about real life/be concerned with the problems of real life	Literary appreciation is based on personal opinions/emotions

Do you think Rita will succeed …?

Students might feel that Rita is too emotional to be able to think in the academic way required to pass exams. On the other hand, she is highly motivated. There is a danger that she will lose her honesty and spontaneity and be afraid to give her own views.

Students will probably understand the fear of voicing one's own opinions because they may differ from those of acknowledged critics. They may also be unwilling to have a favourite piece of literature or music analysed because this might take away some of its pleasure.

5. Frank

● Answer

– *Frank has split up from his wife.*

– *Frank is ironic, even sarcastic (his remarks about his wife and Julia). He seems to be bitter about women.*

– *Now he lives with a former student, Julia*

– *He does not like himself very much. He think he is shallow ('there's less to me than meets the eye' (p. 28, ll.16/17).*

– *He is not sure that he is doing a worthwhile job because he is not convinced about the value of education (his comment on Rita's story about the bird).*

– *He is attracted to Rita and even feels he might have married her once (p. 29).*

Homework

Students prepare scene 3.

A7
Act I, scene 3: housing in Britain

Video: Rita's home life

After scene 2 the video includes additional information about Rita's home life, which contributes greatly to an understanding of her situation. It should be shown from the point where Rita is walking home past the gas works to the end of the wall-breaking scene, which finishes with a kiss. It is enough if learners simply watch and try to understand the gist of it. They should be informed that the area where Rita and Denny live is typical of the older working-class districts in the industrial towns and cities of the north. Today many of them have been demolished and replaced by more modern council house estates. The extract on housing in

exercise 1 gives additional information about housing in Britain and about the popularity of D. I. Y. (Do It Yourself), illustrated by Denny's home improvements.

1. Housing

● Answer

Students will have no difficulty in allotting Rita and Denny to the second rung of the ladder, the terraced house. The English term can be roughly translated as 'Reihenhaus', but refers to the older type of building shown in the video and mainly found in run-down areas of northern industrial towns and cities.

Judging by the conversation on p. 19, l.5–8, Frank has a better type of house out in the suburbs (Formby). It is probably a semi-detached one (also known as a 'semi').

2. Interrupting Rita

The video scenes illustrated how Rita's studies are interrupted by Denny's improvements to the house. Rita's environment is unsympathetic to her ambitions and people will not understand her need for privacy and quiet. She will be constantly interrupted by relatives, neighbours and friends. Working in groups or pairs, students try to imagine the nature of these interruptions.

● Answer

– *My sister is getting married and she needed my help/wanted me to go with her to buy her dress/…*

– *My mother asked me to go round for a cup of tea.*

– *A neighbour wanted me to babysit.*

etc.

A8
Act I, scene 3: writing literary criticism; 'good' literature

1. How to write literary criticism

● Answer

a) *Because she made too many references to a writer of pulp fiction instead of to authors of good quality literature.*

Working in groups, students compile a list of conventions for writing literary criticism. They are then given the list on p. 50 and asked to compare it with their own.

Techniques of Literary Criticism

The most common way of responding to literature is through an essay in which you are asked to 'Discuss…', 'Compare…', 'Give a personal response…'. Essays like this are called *literary criticism*, and you need to be able to analyse the text and describe your response. There are certain basic techniques for writing in this way.

1 Answer the question
2 Write in an appropriate style
3 Support your opinions with evidence

1 Answer the question

In order to answer the question successfully you need to be absolutely clear about what you are being asked to do. The question will definitely **not** ask you to retell the storyline. This is the biggest mistake GCSE[1] students make – retelling the story rather than answering the question.

Start by underlining or writing out the key words from the question, and then make notes. In your notes you should be writing down the key points you will make in the course of your essay.

Everyone has their own preferred style of note making – some use lists of points; some use spider-diagrams. Whichever format you use, be systematic: try to cover all the main points. Do not write much at this stage – you are simply looking to list the key points of your essay.

2 Write in an appropriate style

Literary criticism usually requires a fairly formal style. That means you should:

• Use Standard English.
• Avoid *elisions* (e.g. isn't, aren't)
• Generally use an impersonal style – but you do not have to avoid saying 'I' or 'me' altogether.
• Use a variety of sentence types.
• Use cohesive devices to add variety and clarity to your writing: *however, although, therefore, then, at first, later… and so on.*
• Show that you are answering the question by echoing its phrasing at the start of new paragraphs.

3 Support your opinions with evidence

One of the most important techniques when writing literature essays is to use quotations to support your ideas.

There are two ways of using quotations:

1 Place long quotations (more than one sentence) in a separate paragraph.
2 Embed short quotations into your own sentences.

(Taken from English to GCSE by G. Barton, by permission of Oxford University Press)

[1]An exam for British pupils

b) Do you think…?
To answer this question students refer to the above guidelines in detail. This will also help them to remember the advice when writing their own essays.

Could she…?
At the moment Rita would not be able to write an acceptable essay. Her way of thinking is disorganised, spontaneous and emotional. She does not yet think systematically enough to be able to stick to the question asked. She would probably write down all sorts of jumbled thoughts.

Would she…?
She cannot use formal language yet. She uses dialect, not Standard English and is probably not used to writing much at all, especially not formal English. She also thinks in a very subjective way, so would tend to use 'I' too often. So far, we have not heard her use much variety of sentence types or cohesive devices. She does not know about the technique of echoing the phrasing of the question at the start of new paragraphs.

Would she support?
Rita has not yet learned to support her opinions with evidence. Her judgements are still highly subjective and not based on any evidence in the text.

c) What does Rita still have to learn?
Rita still has to learn to be more selective (pp. 30/31) and more discerning (p. 32, l.5). She has to learn to recognise the difference in quality between various literary works.

2. How do you tell?

Frank is confused and embarrassed because Rita asks him to explain something which he takes for granted. People in his academic circles have 'always known' what constitutes good literature.

Students think about how they themselves recognise good literature by comparing it with pulp fiction. To do this they complete a diagram, showing which elements are usually found in popular best sellers (also written best-seller). They can either draw in additional packets and jugs, or simply write the words in. After comparing their answers with each other they can be given the following definition from a guide preparing British students for English literature exams.

One of the main differences between popular best sellers and literature is that the main purpose of best sellers is to entertain the reader: to amuse, excite or to shock. They don't usually set out to challenge the way the reader thinks about the world. Good literature sets out to make you think. The author will be attempting to put across a serious point. Of course, good literature can also be humorous, entertaining and shocking. It may even use the same genres as the best seller: romances, science fiction and detective stories can all be found in books which are generally agreed to be 'great' literature.

(Letts Study Guide. GCSE English. National Curriculum. Key Stage 4. Letts Educational 1995).

Students should realize that their tastes have been channelled by people such as parents, librarians and teachers. They have also been taught to recognise good quality writing by learning how to analyse literature.

The following quotation can serve as a stimulus for discussion.

A general problem in all knowledge concerns the extent to which our observations disturb, destroy or create what it is that we are studying. With literature and criticism this problem is particularly acute: their study today is inescapably centred in academic departments of literature, but these same departments are influential in defining what we see as literature, how it is to be critically studied, and even (to a more limited extent) how it is to be written. Is literary criticism then an activity that has been created by the academy and has little or no relationship with the manner in which 'ordinary' (or 'common') readers read?
An adequate response to this question has to be more sophisticated than a simple 'yes' or 'no'. To start with, it needs to be pointed out that there can be few – perhaps no – 'ordinary readers' whose reading habits have not been at least partly formed through education. This has always been true in a general sense: someone always has to teach us to read. But in the present century the forming of reading habits has become more and more intimately linked with the educational system. Not only do most of us start reading literature at school, but our teachers have been trained in colleges and universities (...)
But is literature independent of literary criticism? Are not our readerly expectations, or reading skills, or very view of what literature is, formed at least in part by literary criticism – particularly

through its association with education? Would the novels and poems that are being written today have been written had no literary criticism been written?

(Jeremy Hawthorn: Unlocking the Text. Edward Arnold, 1987, pp. 7–8)

3. Russell on 'good' literature

Russell himself is highly critical of the elitist way in which literature is dealt with (c.f. A3, 1). Through Rita he exposes the fragile basis of assumptions about 'good' literature. He questions the absolute status of great authors, which is created by what he calls the 'literature industry'.

● Answer
– *In Russell's view, the following are responsible for propagating a 'high art culture': a literature industry, an opera industry, a theatre industry, the spokesmen, shapers, makers, the writers about it, the communicators about it, for example magazines about the theatre and theatre critics.*
– *These people 'think that art is only for the few' (Russell), that is, for the highly educated minority.*

Can you understand…?
Students can use vocabulary from the interview to help them with their explanations.
Frank finds Rita refreshing because her reactions to literature have not been shaped by anyone. She does not react in the approved or orthodox way because she does not know anything about literature or the literature industry. Frank's students and colleagues are probably unable to react to literature in the emotional, honest way that Rita does because they know what they are supposed to think. Rita is also probably more genuinely interested in literature than Frank's other students.

Does Frank reject…?
Frank does not reject pulp fiction, but suggests that Rita should be aware of its place in the literary hierarchy: pulp fiction is not usually studied, but simply read for enjoyment.

Homework
Students read scene 4 and prepare exercise 1 of A 9.

A 9
Working class culture; newspapers and social class

1. Working class culture
The class aspect of the discussion is now focussed on 'working class culture' in particular. Russell feels strongly that the working class is being denied access to many aspects of the national culture. Because of

expectations about their tastes and abilities, also because they themselves are very reluctant to change and to try new things, they only have limited access to cultural products. Unlike many who write on 'working class culture', Russell refuses to romanticise about it.

In scene 4 he uses Rita as a mouthpiece for his own ideas.

● Answer

pp. 35/36:

– *The working class have no culture.*
– *Working class people spend their lives trying to get from one day to the next/living from day to day, often with the help of alcohol and pills (sedatives).*
– *Working class people are too proud to admit they have problems.*
– *The working class think they have culture.*
– *Materially, the working class are quite well off, but they realize that something is lacking in their lives. (Today the so-called 'traditional working class' is no longer well off, but is gradually sinking into an 'underclass').*
– *There is a lot of violence, which shows that something is wrong.*
– *The people who are supposed to represent the working class (certain newspapers, ITV and the trade unions) only concentrate on material values. But this does not give meaning to life.*
– *The choices which the working class have are only material ones and even these are manipulated by ITV and the papers.*

Does Frank share…?

No. Frank does not know anything about working class life and is not interested in it. He probably has a romanticised view of it, possibly formed by what he has read about it in novels (c.f. D. H. Lawrence). Even after Rita has painted a depressing picture of working class culture he cannot see anything wrong with it as long as people are happy (p. 35, ll.35/36).

Russell is probably suggesting that the middle classes have certain stereotyped concepts of working class life. Because they have no direct contact with such people they rely on what they read. Rita's description destroys any romanticised images. Again, Russell is showing the barriers which exist between the classes. He is also implying that the better educated are not interested in those less privileged than themselves.

Why…hates politics?

Rita probably hates politics because she sees that politicians are not interested in changing the situation of the working class in any fundamental way. She probably thinks that they, too, try to suggest that the answer to the problems of the working class is to simply give them more money.

Additional information:

Russell once expressed his ideas on 'working class culture' in an interview:

"But is there a pure working-class culture? No, I don't think of it as pure because its a hybrid culture really…I am aware of, without really being able to define it, the difference between a high art culture and what we, for the sake of convenience, call a working-class culture. And it's easier to define a high art culture than it is to describe the hybrid, working-class culture. High art is refined art – opera houses, poetry books, concert halls, theatres. Just as I don't want the class division, I really don't want those cultural divisions. I want the concert hall, and the opera stage, and the poetry book to mean just as much to Joe as they do to Joseph…How you ever achieve that, I don't know, but it would be better if you didn't have a high art culture and a polarized working-class culture."

(Jones, C. N.: Populism, The Mainstream Theatre, and the Plays of Willy Russell. UMI Dissertation Information Services. Ann Arbor, Michigan 1989, pp. 320–321)

2. 'Only connect'

Working in groups and using Rita's description on pp. 36–37 as a basis, students try to fill in the diagram. Depending on the class, help can be given in the form of vocabulary aids.

● Answer

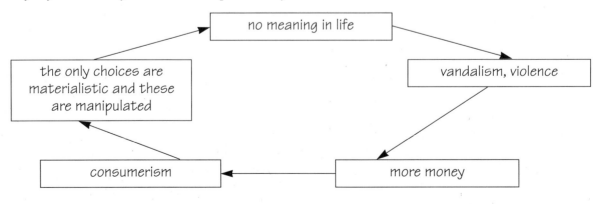

Additional information:

Forster used the motto *only connect* to introduce his novel, *Howards End*. He was referring to the process by which separate elements combine to make a whole and explained it by drawing a parallel with music: 'When the symphony is over we feel that the notes and tunes composing it have been liberated, they have found in the rhythm of the whole their individual freedom' (E. M. Forster: Aspects of the Novel. Edward Arnold, London, 1927, p. 216).

In *Howards End* the motto refers to the interplay of seemingly opposite forces in life – poverty and wealth, culture and ignorance, love and hate. Forster himself describes these various levels as the *poetry and prose* of life. He was very much aware of the interplay between spiritual and material needs and believed that the artist should have a solid financial base to his life. In the novel these opposing strands are eventually unified through one figure, Margaret Schlegel. She represents a bridge connecting three different social classes and also the material and spiritual elements of life.

How does Rita…?
Rita sees education as a means of escape. It will help her to find real meaning in life by giving her more choices than only materialistic ones.

3. Newspapers and social class
Students should not be given the sources of the articles until they have had the chance to work out the differences between them for themselves.
'Naked Brits'…' / 'Crash girl…': *The Sun, 2/4/97*
'Maggie…': *The Sun, 18/3/97*
'Blair…': *The Independent, 18/3/97*

● Answer
'Blair…', 'Maggie…'
– *'Maggie…': more eye-catching because of larger headlines and different kinds of type; text broken up into small segments, so easy to read; personal style.*
– *'Blair…': impersonal, more analytic, longer sentences (readers presumed to be used to longer, more difficult sentences).*
After this analysis students are informed as to the sources of each text.

Which of these papers…?
All the articles except 'The Independent' are probably of the type Rita mentions: 'Crash girl…' is sensational and plays on the readers' emotions; 'Naked Brits' is titillating.

4. Choices
After summarising the extract students should link it to Rita's attempts to break out of the narrow confines of her working class environment.

● Answer
Rita recognises that the working class is manipulated by the mass media, 'ITV an' the papers tell them what to spend it on…covered up' (p. 36, ll.15–21). She also realises that the choices, although many, are really very narrow – quantity as opposed to quality. In scene 1, for instance, she said that life should really offer more choices than which club to go to or which clothes to buy (p. 24). She sees that manipulation by the mass media contributes to depriving the working class of real choices, 'there's no meaning…they know they've got nothin'' (p. 36, ll.3, 9). This reflects the author's own strong views about how the working class is deprived of better quality choices (c.f. A 4, 2; A 8, 3).

Homework
Students read scene 5 and do exercise 10,1.

A 10
Act I, scene 5: Denny's reactions; a woman's role; Frank

1. Denny's reactions
Look at…

● Answer
– *Denny does not like Rita studying at home (p. 33, ll.24/25).*
– *He tried to stop her going to her class (p. 36, l.28). He wanted her to go out with him and his friends instead. Rita thinks he feels threatened because she is doing something unusual. He is afraid because she is becoming a stronger person. He wants her to behave like himself, in order to reinforce his own values and justify his own way of life. He feels she is betraying him and her social origins by no longer accepting their kind of life. He is afraid of change.*
– *He wants her to have a baby (p. 38, ll.14/15).*
– *He resents her studies so much that he has burnt her books and homework (p. 38, l.16).*
– *He is jealous of what Frank can give her ('room to breathe', p. 39, l.4). He may even suspect that they are having an affair (p. 39, l.11).*
– *He cannot understand that Rita wants more meaningful choices in life than materialistic ones (p. 40, ll.3–8). (Compare the lack of real choice in newspapers, see A 10, 3.)*

What do you think…?
Students speculate as to how the story will develop. They may suggest that Rita will give up her course

altogether. She might write to Frank and explain, or she might make an excuse and offer to pay for the books. Frank might accept this, or he might not. If he does he might go and see her. These speculations can be used as a starting point for written or oral work, for example to write Rita's letter to Frank or to make up a telephone conversation in which she explains what has happened.

Video: The video includes scenes showing Denny's reactions to Rita's studying, which contribute greatly to the understanding of the play. Students watch the scene starting with Denny in the garden with his bonfire, up to the close-up of Rita after he has burnt her books.

2. A woman's place is in the home
What do you think…?

● Answer
The man is probably saying something like 'What do you think you're doing? When are you going to stop all this reading? When will things get back to normal? You're neglecting the housework with all this reading and I have to help out. Don't you think I've enough to do? I can't understand you. Haven't you got everything you want here at home? etc.

Does the cartoon suggest…?
Using the cartoon as a stimulus students can add a few more aspects to Denny's objections, for instance that his wife might not do as much housework any more, might not cook as much etc.

How does Rita feel…?
Rita understands Denny's feelings and is sorry for him ('I see him lookin'…, p. 39, l.21). But she knows she has already changed and can no longer go back to what she was before. She realises that Denny is so fixed in his ways and in his thinking that he is incapable of understanding her needs.

Make up…
Using their notes and also their ideas about the cartoon, students either write or make up an oral argument between Rita and Denny.

3. A metaphor

● Answer
The course of reading, knowledge and education represents life itself to Rita: 'room to breathe. Y'… feed me (p. 39, l.4), providing me with life itself. He wants to take life away from me, rockin' the coffin (trying to put life into something which is dead. This is a reference to the saying 'rocking the boat', which means trying to change the way things are normally done, rebelling against tradition. By using the word 'coffin' instead of

boat Rita is implying that her old way of life resembles death), it's given me more life… I'm alive' (p. 39, l.34–p. 40, l.1).

Video: The video shows Rita watching an Open University programme on TV late at night. (Some courses broadcast accompanying programmes on the radio and BBC2.) The clip helps students to understand the difficulties she has studying at home. The scene is shown from the point where the TV screen appears, up to where Rita stands breathless in front of Frank. (Frank: What is it? What's wrong?) Students speculate as to what can have happened.

Homework
Read scene 6 to find out what has happened; do exercises A 10, 4 and 5.

4. Frank, the poet

● Answer
Frank drinks in order to forget or suppress his frustration about his teaching, his poetry, the way literature is dealt with by the so-called 'experts' (the "literature industry") and his personal life. He does not really think he has anything important to say, 'booze… makes one believe… something' (p. 41, ll.8–10). He realises that he cannot write poetry which really expresses things in a powerful way. Instead, he tried to write 'literature', or the sort of work which would be acceptable to literary critics and could be studied and 'appreciated' by students.

Students can be reminded of Russell's own highly critical attitude to what he called the "literature industry" (see the interview with Russell in A8, 3). The following distinction between writing 'literature' and being a 'creative writer' is a useful basis for further discussion:

We may still speak of the literature on a particular topic, or ask for literature describing a particular product, but, in most usages, literature has come to indicate a distinct kind of writing with a particular significance in society. 'She is literate' indicates that a person is a fluent reader and writer. 'She is a creative writer' indicates that a person writes from her own thoughts and imagination; the results may be poetry or advertising, etc. 'She writes literature', on the other hand, seems an odd formulation, the more recognizable phrase is 'she reads literature'. Our unease about the first formulation is because literature depends upon more than an individual act of writing. It requires an act of what is generally called criticism. Among other things this serves to place the writing on some kind of scale of values and declares it worth reading.

(The Open University: The changing experience of women. Unit 5. Milton Keynes, 1983, p. 7).

5. Frank, the cynic
By rephrasing Rita's comments in a more fluent way students become more aware of her difficulties in expressing herself. This also prepares the ground for a comparison with her improved command of the language towards the end of the play.

● Answer
The student's suggestions should show their understanding of Frank's cynicism, e. g.
You never really say what you're thinking/show your real feelings, do you? You always put on a/hide your feelings behind a cynical facade.

A 11
Act I, scene 6: Macbeth; tragedy; the dinner party

1. Macbeth

● Answer
Rita tells Frank that she went to the theatre because she 'wanted to find out' (p. 45, l.2). This reminds us of her telling him 'I wanna know' in scene 1 (p. 12, l.17, c. f. A 3, 4). She wants to find out what she has missed. She has decided to read the kind of books and go to the kind of plays she would have rejected before. She expected to be bored by Shakespeare (p. 44, l.37).

Can you remember…?
Students can discuss in how far the experience of seeing plays at the theatre is different from reading them or watching them on TV. They could discuss whether the theatre has a function for people with little or no contact with art.

What does Rita's reaction…?
Rita still reacts to literature in a completely emotional way.

Additional information:

Rita's first visit to the theatre echoes an important event in the author's own life. When he first started to go to the theatre he disliked it because it seemed so far removed from his own experience (c. f. notes on A 2,6). But the early seventies was a key period for regional drama. Until then audiences were offered well-tried classics such as Priestley's *An Inspector Calls*. A group of young directors in Liverpool, Birmingham, Stoke and other cities injected new life into the theatre by encouraging new, local playwrights. This was the turning-point for Russell. He enjoyed this new type of play so much that he decided to study drama at a teacher's training college. While he was there he decided to become a playwright and to write for working class audiences. Indeed, he is remarkable because no other British playwright has ever had such a series of successes all dealing with the lives of the working class.

Russell once explained his views on working class attitudes to the theatre: "I'm not putting down the bourgeois plays. I love many of them. But they are bourgeois plays because they are written by the bourgeoisie for the bourgeoisie. By this time[1], you have a generation of working-class people who have never known the habit of going to the theatre, who have been totally intimidated, who would never dare to presume to go to these places. By the time we get to Victorian times, the working-class man in England was a white nigger. It's as simple as that. He couldn't go to the theatre. He probably wouldn't want to, given what was on offer. If he was represented on the stage, it was as a bumbling oaf or as a patronized, servile jack-the-lad. His role was never examined on the stage… Of course, what happened was in the twenties – and thirties and forties – you still had this middle-class stranglehold on the theatre, excluding whole sections of our society."

[1] mid-nineteenth century
(Jones, C. N., pp. 312–313)

2. Tragedy
Before defining 'tragedy' in literary terms it is helpful to show how the type of newspapers Rita reads (c. f. A 9) colours her perception of 'tragedy'.

● Answer
Rita would probably regard the following headlines as 'tragedies': Six-year-old…, Couple…, Tragedy…

How would you paraphrase…?

● Answer
The events which Rita would describe as 'tragic' may be terribly sad, but they are not 'tragic' in a literary sense: a perm that does not come out right, an angry customer, a man killed by a falling tree. Frank defines 'tragedy' in literary terms: pre-ordained events/things that cannot be avoided or changed. Tragic characters take inevitable steps towards their own doom; flaws in their characters dictate their end/they bring on their own doom. (The flaw in Macbeth's character was his ambition to be king.)

55

3. The dinner party

Students work in groups. From what they know of Denny they will presume that he refuses to go and that the two quarrel. The conversations can first be written down, then performed in front of the class.

Video: The corresponding video clip begins with Rita going into her living-room and asking Denny if he is going to change his mind about the dinner party and ends with Rita in the pub (the first pub scene). It includes a very poignant shot of Rita standing outside Frank's house, looking in. The shot can be frozen while students imagine her thoughts. The clip is also valuable for the pictures of everyday life and especially because it helps learners to visualise the kind of pressure Rita is up against.

Homework:
Students read scene 7.

A12
Act I, scene 7: Rita's identity crisis

1. Rita's reactions

● Suggested answers
I don't know if I can go in there. They're all educated people. I won't belong. They'll laugh at me. I won't know what to talk about.
Students can describe situations where they themselves have felt like outsiders. Those in a similar situation, for instance, would be handicapped people, someone who has gone to live in a new area or someone with a different way of life or different view to the majority.

2. In the pub

Some students will have Denny telling the truth ('She's gone to that stupid university' etc.), others will decide that he will make excuses such as 'She has a headache' or 'She doesn't feel well'.

Rita did not...
Students make up a written or spoken dialogue. Rita would probably make up some excuse, such as 'I got the date wrong' or 'I decided to come here instead'. How the conversation develops depends on whether Denny accepts her explanation or not.

Was Frank right...?
Some students will believe that Frank acted in all innocence and really believed that Rita and Denny would enjoy the evening. Others will probably regard him as tactless and shallow, unable to see that he had put Rita in a very embarrassing position. He should have known that it would cause conflict between her and her husband, also that Rita would feel very uncomfortable among his friends.

3. In between

Students work in pairs or groups.

● Answer
The diagrams will differ, but should show that Denny and the people in the pub form a group, as do Julia and the dinner party guests. Rita and Frank are outsiders. Frank does not belong to the normal, middle class academic culture. He stresses that it is Julia who had planned the dinner party (p. 47, l.28).

Some students might also put Rita's mother slightly outside her group (p. 51, ll.5 ff.).

As the learners compare their diagrams they explain them and defend their decisions. One possible diagram would be the one below.

Explain...
Using Rita's own words as a guide (p. 51), students explain that Rita feels she no longer belongs to her old environment. Yet she does not feel at home with Frank's circle of friends either.

4. Rita's decision

● Answer
In the pub Rita's mother started to cry and said 'We could sing better songs than those' (p. 51, ll.9/10). Whereas Denny tries to pretend that nothing has happened, Rita understands her mother's frustration and becomes even more determined that the same thing will not happen to her. She decides she will go on trying to give her life more meaning. She realises that this means breaking away even more from her old environment. This will be painful, but it is more important to her to take on responsibility for her own life, to be able to have more choices in what to do with her life.

Rita's reactions
She is even more determined to go on. She does not want to become as unhappy and frustrated as her mother.

Denny's reactions
He understands his mother-in-law's frustration and disappointment, but prefers to ignore it; pretends

nothing has happened. He does not want to think about problems, but prefers a facade of happiness to the truth. He does not have the courage to try to change things.

What is… mother?
Rita's mother is a dramatic foil to Rita. She feels disappointed and frustrated at the emptiness of her life, but does not have enough will-power to change it. She allows Denny to cheer her up and goes on pretending that everything is all right. This contrast underlines Rita's actions, making them more forceful. Rita becomes even more determined to change her life while she is still young, before she becomes like her mother.

Do you…?
Students can discuss Denny in groups or as a whole class.

5. Why not sing the old song?

Does Frank understand…?
No. First he suggests that she needs a psychiatrist 'if you can't believe…' (p. 50, ll. 20/21). Then he asks why, if the course is causing so many problems, she does not give it up, stay with her family and join in the singing. He does not understand that this is no longer possible for her ('You think I can, don't you?' p. 51, l.1). Unlike Denny, she cannot pretend that everything is fine and that she is happy.
Russell could be suggesting that the middle class, especially academics, do not know anything about the lives of the less privileged.

Homework:
Students read scene 8.

A13
Act I, scene 8: Rita's decision

1. Betrayed

● Answer
The tramp is being ironic. The idea of betraying one's class usually refers to the working class. It is normally regarded as a point of honour for the working class to remain loyal to their origins (as does, for instance, Denny). The tramp, however, would have no such scruples about abandoning his social status for a more privileged one. His use of the word 'traitor' echoes Denny's accusation that Rita has betrayed him by rejecting his way of life and that of his class. Rita understands this and concedes that he is right, from his point of view. But she has to go on. She feels it is more important not to betray herself, which means that she has to try to live up to her potential.

Additional information:
The theme of working class individuals trying to break out of a repressive family and community runs through Russell's plays, as is explained in the following quotation.

'Willy Russell's plays make dynamic use of Liverpool dialect and are full of scouse wit but the author does not have a rose-tinted view of Liverpool or 'Liverpool working class people'. In fact, the plays are very critical of the tribal, bigoted and conservative elements in Liverpool life because these attitudes can prevent individuality developing. Most of Russell's plays could be seen as a battle between an individual with a strong sense of his or her own identity, and a working class family or community which represses anyone escaping from the herd. In fact, 'imprisoning circumstances' really means a working class Liverpool world which has lost its value to the escaper.
(Gill, J.: Willy Russell and His Plays. Countyvise, Birkenhead 1996, pp. 109–111)

Video: This sense of imprisonment is also illustrated in a sequence from the video. It begins with the wedding of Rita's sister, Sandra, during which Denny issues his ultimatum (text p. 51, ll. 29–31), and ends with Denny walking off, leaving Rita alone. It shows the expectations of Rita's family and community that she should accept the traditional role of women, have children and stay at home.

2. Decisions
Working in pairs and using the sentence structures provided, students describe Rita's and Frank's situations. Each then reads out his or her sentences to the other.

● Answer
RITA
Rita has to decide whether to / if she wants to go on studying / with her studies.
If she goes on, her marriage will break up / she will lose her husband / her whole life will change /…
She is sure that she wants to go on.
She has already made the/her decision.

FRANK
Frank has to decide whether to / if he wants to go on teaching Rita. If he goes on, he will have to change her way of thinking / destroy something in her/destroy her honest, emotional, unconventional way of thinking / response to literature / make her suppress her spontaneity /…
He is not sure if he wants to do that / go on.
He has not made his decision yet.

Rita's essay makes it clear to Frank, once again, that she cannot yet pass exams because her thinking is too emotional and not structured enough. However, he values her honest, unconventional reactions to literature. Unlike his other students, she does not talk about it in a cold, rational, analytical way. He knows that if she is to pass exams he will have to make her suppress her spontaneity.

Does Rita understand…?
No. Rita cannot see Frank's problem at all.
– *Frank wants Rita to go on reacting to literature in a personal, emotional way/go on being herself/…*
– *Rita wants Frank to teach her to pass exams/to be like the other students/…*

How do…?
The students' suggestions can be noted down and referred back to as the play progresses.

3. Rita goes to her mother's
In pairs or groups students make up a conversation between Rita and her mother. Some may decide that, on the basis of her mother's behaviour in the pub, she will be sympathetic and encourage her daughter. Others may feel that tradition and accepted codes of behaviour are more important to her than individual happiness, so she might blame Rita for the break-up of her marriage and might try to persuade her to go back home and forget about studying.
Depending on the class, vocabulary aids or even a defective dialogue might have to be provided.

Homework
Read Act II, scene 1; do exercise A 14, 1.

A 14
Act II, scene 1: after summer school

1. Summer school
As part of her OU course Rita has been to a summer school in London.

● Answer
– *Rita has changed her style of dressing.*
– *She has made new friends.*
– *She has probably experienced life in the big city for the first time, without anyone to restrict her.*
– *She has been to more theatres.*
– *She has become more self-confident about expressing her views on literature.*
– *She has learned a lot more about literature, especially Chekhov.*

Do you think…?
Rita is probably wrong in thinking that Frank would have been proud of her, because this is what he was afraid of. He did not want her to only discusses literature from the point of view of literary theories, without becoming personally involved with it.

2. Frank's reactions

Video: Besides using the text, students can also be given exercise 2 as a pre-viewing task to the corresponding video clip. It begins with Frank and Rita walking across the lawn as she leaves for summer school and ends with him dropping her outside a row of houses, after her return.
The film clearly shows Frank's disappointment when Rita rejects his present of cigarettes and also when she has already read Blake's poems. It also shows the pressure which Rita exerts on him by giving him a pen, expressly for the purpose of writing poetry.

● Answer
The answer can be written in table form. It may be necessary to provide vocabulary aids.

Changes in Rita	Frank's thoughts
– *Appearance.*	– *She looks like any other student now.*
– *Experiences in London.*	– *Oh, God! Just like all the others.*
– *She has stopped smoking.*	– *Oh no. Now she's become health-conscious. And I bought her the cigarettes.*
– *She has a new flatmate.*	– *I didn't know about that. She doesn't tell me everything any more. (Trish is short for Patricia.)*
– *She is trying to influence him, trying to get him to write poetry again. Before, she accepted him as he was.*	– *Oh no. Now she's trying to make me write poetry. Why can't she just leave me alone. I'm not a poet.*
– *She criticises his drinking (p. 59, l.10).*	– *She didn't use to criticise my drinking. She even had one with me sometimes. Now she's trying to reform me.*
– *She is already familiar with Blake.*	– *Oh no. How disappointing. I've been looking forward to seeing her reactions to Blake.*

Comment on…

Frank can see how Rita has changed already. He knows that as she becomes an 'expert' on literature he will dislike her more and more. When Rita asks if he means what he says he gives her a superficial, flippant answer. He knows that she would not understand his fears and that, in any case, he can no longer stop her from becoming a 'proper' student, with all that this entails.

Can you explain…?

In Act I, scene 1 Frank said that Rita was the first breath of fresh air that had been in his room for years. He meant that he found her refreshing in the stuffy, airless atmosphere of the university, or higher education in general. Now, however, he no longer sees her as a breath of fresh air. It is symbolical that she cannot open the window. The room has had all the fresh air it will ever get. There will never be another student like Rita and the old Rita has gone.

3. Songs of Innocence and Experience

● Answer

Russell's choice of Blake's collection symbolises Rita's progress from innocence to experience in the sense that she is no longer ignorant about literature and literary criticism. It could also be seen as a warning that she might not be able to realise her dreams or that they may turn sour.

Homework

Students read scenes 2–4.

A15
Act II, scenes 2–4: Frank; reversed roles

1. Frank's feelings

This exercise can be done in pair work, students taking it in turns to ask each other a question. Alternatively, it can take the form of a 'hot chair' session in which one student takes the part of Frank and the others – either the whole class or the other groups members – put their questions to him. Students can take it in turns to play Frank.

● Answer
The following points should be covered:

BEING LATE
– *Rita was late for her class. This suggests that Frank's lessons are not so important to her any more. First she said it was 'unavoidable' (p. 62, l.19), but later she told Frank that she actually arrived early and talked to some students (p. 63, ll.14/15). Frank will probably be offended that she preferred talking to the students to keeping her appointment with him.*

UNNATURAL VOICE/TRISH
– *Frank dislikes Rita's unnatural voice and will probably feel that she is too much under Trish's influence (p. 63, ll.1/2). Besides copying Trish's voice, Rita also takes over her opinions (p. 67).*

THE OTHER STUDENTS
– *Frank sees that Rita is now self-confident enough to go and talk to the other students. When she started her course she would not have dared to approach them. She was in awe of them (p. 63, ll.17–23). He is probably afraid of losing her when she talks about going on holiday with them. He is also jealous of Tyson (p. 64, ll.26 ff.).*
– *Frank feels that Rita shows off (p. 64, l.6).*

RITA'S ESSAY
– *Frank had been saving Blake's poetry to read with Rita. It means of lot to him and he thought she would see it in the same way as he does. He thought that, like him, she would react to it emotionally, without over-complicating it with literary analysis. He is disappointed when he sees that she has taken over trendy, second-hand opinions instead of expressing her own feelings (p. 67/68). Now he thinks she has become just like all his other students, giving him the accepted, second-hand opinions which they read in books on literary criticism.*

'BORING, INSIGNIFICANT DETAIL/TRAPPED'
– *Frank sees that Rita is no longer as interested in other people and in life in general as she used to be. All she seems to want to talk about is literature. In scene 4 she describes her change of job as a 'boring, insignificant detail' (p. 70, ll.5/6) and 'irrelevant rubbish' (p. 70, ll.10/11).*
– *Frank will probably be very hurt by Rita's comment that the students are 'not trapped' because he himself feels trapped. He really wants to be a poet and does not fit into established academic life (compare his statement about creating 'literature', p. 41, l.20). He would prefer to let students react to literature in their own, personal way, instead of forcing them to judge it by the accepted standards of literary criticism. It is because he feels trapped by his job that he drinks and puts on a cynical, flippant facade. Rita does not understand this and it would no longer interest her.*
– *Frank is also very hurt when Rita explains that she has to continue with her tutorials because of her exams. He shows his disappointment by moving further away from her and by his comment, 'I'd rather you spared me that' (p. 71, ll.10/11). He also suggests that she is now incapable of recognising what really matters, meaning that she is no longer interested in other people and does not see his problems.*

59

In Act I, scene 5, when Rita told Frank that her marriage was breaking up, he warned her, 'When art and literature begin to take the place of life itself, perhaps it's time to…' (p. 39, ll. 28/29). At the time, Rita chose art and literature in preference to her husband because they represented life to her. She was trying to escape from a deadening environment. But now that she has managed to escape, art and literature really do seem to have become more important to her than life itself – more important, that is, than her relationships with other people. She has forgotten why she started the course, to discover herself. She now only appears to be interested in literary criticism for its own sake. She seems to have completely suppressed her past life, as if it never existed. Hairdressing is now a 'boring detail'.

2. Rita's essay

● Answer
Rita rejects Frank's criticism. She suspects that his pride is hurt because she did not echo his own opinions ('there's nothing of your views in there', p. 67, ll. 35/36).

Is Frank right…?
Some students might feel that Frank is right to insist on Rita expressing her own views, others may find him unfair because he is criticising the very thing he asked her to do: 'you told me not to have a view … conclusions' (p. 68, ll. 5 ff.).

Additional information:
The Blossom (p. 67) is one of the *Songs of Innocence.* The following interpretation of it can be read out to illustrate the kind of literary appreciation which Frank dislikes and which he fears Rita will begin to produce.

> "It has been suggested that this is a love poem imbued with passion and movement, almost as if Blake's unconscious or subconscious has been responsible for those additional dimensions of suggestions which are so original and intense in their verbal power, even, one is tempted to suggest, in the innocence of their verbal power. Sparrows are traditionally associated with happiness, and robins occasionally with sadness. Note the regularity and the variations, the change of mood conveyed by the use of 'Merry' as distinct from 'Pretty', and the economical nature of both the imagery 'swift as arrow' and the description."
>
> (Brodie's Notes: William Blake. Songs of Innocence and Experience. McMillan 1992)

Compare…
In Act I, scene 2 Rita criticises school for spoiling the students' enjoyment of things by making them think about them and analyse them. But now she, too, is becoming like the teachers. She cannot enjoy Blake's poem on a simple, uncomplicated level, as Frank wants her to.

How do…?
Students discuss in how far analysing literature enhances or spoils their pleasure.

Video: The video clip corresponding to scenes 2 – 4 sticks very closely to the text. It begins with Rita walking through the rain and entering Frank's study and ends with him leaving the bistro.
The sequence showing Frank's lecture is interesting because of his indirect, ironic references to the changes in Rita: "What does it benefit a man if he gaineth the whole of literature and loseth his soul?" He goes on to quote Rita's definition of assonance ('getting the rhyme wrong') in a bitter jibe against the literary establishment, which takes itself so seriously but, he feels, fails to teach people how to appreciate literature properly. His bitter, ironic tone is also directed against himself, for he is a part of the literary establishment.
Frank's feelings are expressed very poignantly when he is talking to Rita in the bistro.

3. Frank's downfall
Students either show sympathy for Frank or they may judge him very harshly.

Make up…
The conversations will probably begin with Rita's enquiry as to what happened at the meeting. They should include the question of what will happen next. Students can draw on both the film and the text for their ideas. Depending on the class, the conversations can be improvised orally in pair work, or written down and then read out in pairs.

Suggested conversation
RITA: *What happened? / What did they say?*
FRANK: *Well, they told me this sort of thing must never happen again and that the consequences could be serious.*
RITA: *Will they sack you?*
FRANK: *God no, that would involve making a decision.*
RITA: *So what will they do?/where do we go from here?*
FRANK: *They suggested I should take a long holiday/a sabbatical for a year – or ten.*
RITA: *When are you going?*
FRANK: *I don't know yet. As soon as I can, I suppose.*

4. Reversed roles

● Answer

RITA	FRANK

is more like (→ ←)

RITA:
- *no longer swears*
- *sits in Frank's chair (p. 66, l.30)*

- *talks about Blake's poem as a literary critic would*

- *rejects 'Rubyfruit Jungle'*
- *no longer dependent on him, tutorials no longer important to her*
- *no longer interested in personal things, does not seem to care about Frank, only wants to discuss literature with him; impersonal, objective.*

FRANK:
- *talks more like Rita used to; 'dead honest' (p. 65, l.4), 'off my cake' (p. 66, l.7); her definition of assonance (p. 66, l.20). The film makes it clear that this is ironic (see above note: video).*
- *reacts to Blake's poem in a simple, emotional way*
- *asks for her views on poetry (p. 71).*
- *enjoyed 'Rubyfruit Jungle'*
- *dependent on her visits*

- *personally interested in Rita, hurt because she no longer tells him everything (p. 70)*

Could Russell...?

After making their own suggestions, students can be given the following interpretation of Russell's role reversal.

> The two characters end up changing places, in many ways, which further suggests the artificiality of the class-based barrier that divides their two existences. By the conclusion of the play it is Frank who is desperate for subjectivity, originality and personality... On the other hand, it is Rita who is making statements like "It becomes a more rewarding poem when you see that it works on a number of levels."
> In short, the message of *Educating Rita* is that these barriers are transcendable, if one has the individual motivation to break them down. It is significant, however, that as Frank 'learns' from Rita he becomes increasingly unacceptable to the university establishment. His new penchant for subjective honesty, coupled with his drinking, leads to his taking a forced sabbatical at the conclusion of the play.
>
> (Jones, C. N., p. 245)

5. Frank's poetry

● Answer
Frank probably asks for Rita's opinion because he is trying to bind her closer to him. Also, he knows that she is usually very honest and does not simply say what is expected.

How...?
Students discuss whether or not Frank and Rita will be able to improve their relationship or whether it will break down. They can also speculate on what will happen after Rita has taken her exam.

Homework
Students read scene 5 and do exercise A 16, 1.

A 16
Act II, scene 5: the quarrel

1. A fine job

● Answer

Describe...
The opinions which Rita gives Frank are not her own, but those of Trish and her friends. (This becomes even clearer in the film.) Frank reacts in an ironic, even sarcastic way. His comment is very bitter. He means that he has turned her into so much of an expert on literature that she now relies more on orthodox, second-hand opinions than on her own. This is exactly what he was afraid would happen. He has made her suppress her emotions and spontaneity. He even implies that he has turned her into a monster (p. 73, ll.7 ff.). Mary Wollstonecraft Shelley (1797–1851), the wife of the poet Shelley, wrote the novel 'Frankenstein' in 1817. It tells the story of how a scientist creates a human being and brings him to life. Lonely and desperate, the creature becomes uncontrollable and the consequences are disastrous.

Educating Rita is an...
Like Russell himself, Rita mistakes the 'veneer' of a cultured educated life for education itself. Like him, she has the 'right' furniture in her room. She does not realise

61

that education means more than copying the life-style and opinions of the educated. Although she can now discuss literature in the established, accepted way, she is no longer directly affected by it, no longer as emotionally involved as she used to be.

Additional information:

Russell himself once commented on Frank's reactions to Rita's opinions in an interview:

'I love him when he says that. He's so positive when he says that because what he's attacking is this woman who has become totally one-dimensional and pseudo-literary. I mean he refers back to the mother's song, doesn't he … Now Rita, when she walks in is wonderful: I mean she's magic; she's a full, potent human being and as Frank says to her very early on: "I don't know why I want to take you through this; it's dangerous territory, you know." And the worst happens. He is forced because, I suppose, he falls in love with her – I mean on a general level – and so he's forced to go along with it. And his forecast comes true … and you've got a Frankenstein-like figure. And that's how I see her when she comes in and talks about his poetry and she says, you know, it's like writing in the way of the 18th-century tradition of wit – and that's rubbish.'

(Glaap, A.-R.: Willy Russell: Educating Rita. Comments and Study Aids. Diesterweg, 1984, p. 24).

2. The Logical Song

● **Answer**

In his job Frank has to be sensible, logical, responsible, practical and dependable. He feels that really he is a poet and that he has become too intellectual, that he analyses things too coldly, too clinically. Perhaps he would like to lead a simpler life and be able to just enjoy things without analysing them too much, like he did when he was young.

Frank is not sure whether the work he is doing has any value. Because he is so unsure he has become cynical. He does not know what he wants in life and has lost his sense of direction. He is going through an identity crisis. Maybe he is thinking of giving up his job and trying to write poetry again.

But Frank knows that if he tells the people around him about his feelings they will reject him and treat him as an outcast. They will be afraid that he wants to challenge the system and question the principles by which they live. So they would prefer him to keep quiet and do and say the orthodox things ('sign up your name'). This would at least make him seem acceptable and respectable, even if it meant that he was unhappy and lived like a vegetable.

Video: The film of scene 5 is very powerful. It begins with Rita going to Frank's house and ends with Frank sitting alone after she has left.

Homework
Do exercise 3; read scenes 6 and 7.

3. The quarrel
The description can be given orally or as a written task, with or without vocabulary aids. Alternatively, it can be turned into a gapped text. This task can be given as homework, if time is short.
The suggestion might be made that Frank and Rita will apologise to each other. If so, students could write and/or act out their apologies in the form of letters or a telephone conversation. It is also possible that a third person might intervene, for instance Trish or Tiger.

● Suggested answers
a) *FRANK:*
I had a quarrel with Rita the other day. She came to see me. I wasn't expecting her. She started off by asking me if I was drunk. Well, that annoyed me for a start!
Then she told me what she thought of my poetry. I had given her some poems that I had written and asked for her opinions on them. You should have heard her. She came out with a lot of pompous, pretentious rubbish. She said they were witty, profound and full of style. But that was not Rita speaking. It was her flatmate, Trish. You don't hear any of Rita's opinions now. She only quotes from other people.
She's changed so much. She used to be so honest. She's just like all the others now. I've created a monster. I never want to see her again. If she comes back I'll just send her away.

b) *RITA:*
I had a quarrel with Frank the other day. A few days ago he gave me some poems he had written and asked for my opinion. I showed them to my flatmate. She said they were more resonant than contemporary poetry. She said you can see a direct line to nineteenth-century traditions.
But, do you know, when I told Frank that, he was angry. He even called me a monster. He doesn't think his poetry is any good. He says it's pretentious, characterless and without style. Then he told me to go away. He said he can't bear me any longer.
I lost my temper then. I really told him what I think of him. He doesn't like me now that I'm educated. He'd prefer me as I was, the little girl who looked up to him and admired everything he said. He doesn't like me because I don't need him. All right then, I'll do it without him. I never want to see him again.

A 17
Act II, scene 5: equal opportunities

1. Education and Social Class

Pick out...

● Answer
The exchange on p. 73, l.29 – p. 74, l.13.

What...?
Through Rita Russell is suggesting that the educated middle classes do not want the working class to have a good education or equal chances, because then they themselves would no longer feel superior.

Do you think...?
Russell seems to be criticising Rita for simply imitating educated people. But he is also implying that Frank is not aware of and does not appreciate his privileged background. Rita attacks him for taking his opportunities for granted and for wasting them. She would have been glad to have had such chances. But Frank does not seem to understand her argument. He can only criticise her. He seems to be completely unaware of the difficulties facing people from Rita's kind of background.

Check...
1. The British class system is changing.	☑
2. In Britain the class system is disappearing.	☐
3. The working class is turning into the middle class.	☐
4. It is difficult to distinguish between the old working class and the new underclass.	☑
5. Russell prefers the working class to the middle class.	☐
6. Russell wants to show that in Britain not everyone has the same educational and cultural opportunities.	☑

Homework
Students read scenes 6 and 7.

A 18
Act II, scenes 6, 7: Frank and Rita; Trish; the ending

1. Frank and Rita

● Answer
Scene 6 reveals that Frank and Rita now have so little contact with each other that he has to ring her at work to tell her the details of her exam. He does not know, either, that she has changed her name back to Susan. Frank is 'taken aback at seeing her' (p. 75, l.12). He obviously had not expected to see her again.

2. Frank, a good teacher?

● Answer
Besides the techniques of literary criticism, Frank has also taught Rita to discipline her mind and to think objectively (c. f. p. 26, ll.18/19: 'if you're going to pass any sort of exam you have to begin to discipline that mind of yours').

Do you agree...?
Students discuss Frank's qualities as a teacher. They may remember that at the beginning he explained one of his principles to Rita, that of allowing learners to find things out for themselves (p. 37, l.11). They should also realise that, although he disliked what Rita was asking him to do, he respected her wishes.
The following extracts from an interview with Russell provides a further stimulus for discussion and shows that the author prefers Frank's way of allowing students to develop and discover things for themselves to a more authoritarian approach. (Russell himself was a teacher for a short time.)

> J. G.   ...would you say that you are definitely against the more authoritarian style of teaching?
>
> W. R.   Totally. It is not the way to convert human beings; to suppress in the human being is to deny it. You've got to acknowledge all the elements of humanity, not try and suppress them, including the base and the vile and potentially the evil.
>
> (John Gill, p. 21)

> W. R.   (Frank is) a real teacher, i. e. he provides the space and the stimulus in which somebody can securely learn, and that's what he does for Rita.
>
> (John Gill, p. 42)

Think about...
Working in groups, students describe the qualities which make a good teacher, using the vocabulary provided.

3. A change in Rita

● Answer
Rita has changed since the quarrel. She has thought about what Frank said and realises that he was right (I just sat... wrong, p. 76, ll.25–27). She sees that she made a mistake. She was so hungry for education and culture that she accepted the opinions of educated people unquestioningly. She thought they must be right simply because of their education. She did not see that some people (like Trish) were just trying to be trendy and that their opinions were empty and superficial ('You think I

ended up... questioned', p. 76, ll.27–30). Rita had become one-dimensional, but now she is more like the warm, direct, honest person she was at the beginning.

Russell himself went through a similar phase to Rita:

"...she feels that she's starving in her present social stratum, that it's arid and that if she moves in this other social stratum it will be some sort of oasis. This was certainly something I felt before I went back to education. I overvalued to a ludicrous extent the idea of education, what, you know, college and higher education was and went through a period being very much like Rita, you know, being very bored and suffering from 'art in the head'. I used to stop people and ask them what they thought of Chekhov which was very boring for them. Poor souls on the buses."

(Willy Russell: Educating Rita. Diesterweg, 1981, p. 95)

This is what Russell himself says about Rita's transformation:

"The human being changes for a while until she can synthesize what she is becoming with what she was".

("Merseyside comes to London again" in: *The Times*, 9. 4. 83)

Most important, perhaps, is Russell's own explanation of his aims:

"At the end of the play what I'm trying to show is somebody who synthesizes the best of what she can gain from literature and what she can get from *Rubyfruit Jungle*... One's talking about a complex woman. It's also, of course, something to do with class. I'm talking about somebody who synthesizes the best of two classes and trying to attack the divisions really in teaching, in education, and in the class system. And so it's the division and it's the elitist way in which literature is dealt with that I really object to.

(Glaap: Comments and Study Aids, p. 22)

4. Trish

Video: Trish's suicide attempt is only briefly alluded to in the text (p. 76, ll.31/32). Her reasons for trying to kill herself are explained in the film. The clip begins with Rita going into the kitchen of the flat she shares with Trish. At the point where Rita finds Trish lying on her bed the shot is frozen and students speculate as to what might have happened *(Trish might have fallen ill / been murdered / committed suicide / tried to kill herself /...)*.
The following sequence of Frank in the bistro, looking for Rita, is omitted so that the question about Trish can be answered immediately: Rita is

sitting at Trish's hospital bed. The clip ends with a close-up of Rita's face. In a listening comprehension exercise students explain what happened and give Trish's reasons: Trish: 'You think I've got everything, don't you? When I listen to poetry and music, then I can live... The rest of the time there's just me, and it's not enough.' Trish needed literature and music to cover up or compensate for an inner emptiness, to give her life some meaning.

Think of...
Rita once told Frank that she finds a lot of her new friends fascinating because they are young and full of energy. They are 'not trapped' (p. 70, l.25), but open to new experiences.
Trish's dramatic function is to make Rita realise that culture and education do not automatically bring happiness. To lead a fulfilled life Rita must do more that talk about literature and copy other people's life-styles. The suggestion is that Rita has simply substituted one mediocre existence for another.

5. Rita's future

Put...

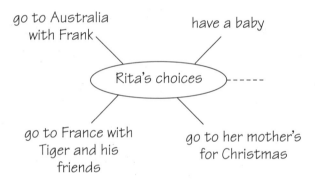

The article about the OU student might trigger off some more ideas, such as become a university lecturer / tutor for the Open University / go on to do research / get a job abroad /...

Write what...
The students' compare and justify their suggestions.

6. The film ending

Video: Rita told Frank that during her exam she thought about what he had said to her (p. 76, ll.25 ff.). This is a suitable point to start watching the final scenes of the video. They begin with a view of the exam room, with papers being handed out.
The shot of Frank watching Rita through a half-open door is frozen and students are asked to imagine his thoughts. Suggestions will probably run along the lines that Frank is glad Rita has finally achieved her aim, but sad because now she really does not need him any more. The closing door could

be seen as a symbol for the end of their relationship. The film is then shown to the end.

Compare...
Students discuss their ideas.

Suggest reasons...
Suggestions might include 'She doesn't love him' or 'Australia is too far away. She wouldn't see her family and friends any more'. The main reason, however, is that Rita has only just freed herself from the demands and expectations of other people. It is only now that she can really begin to take decisions about her own life. So she is not ready to commit herself to any one course of action. As she herself says, "I'll make a decision. I'll choose" (p. 77, l.28).
Students can write their own endings.

7. Choices
Students will probably argue that it does not really matter what Rita does. The main thing is that she now has more interesting alternatives than before she got herself an education.

Russell himself gave his point of view in two interviews:

J. G.   What is 'Educating Rita' about?
W. R.   What the film and the play are about is not really somebody who has to be educated but about somebody who had to arrive at a point in her life where she had more control over her life, more choice. She says 'I don't know how I'll exercise that choice, I might have a baby. I might go back to me mother's, I might go to Australia'. Her actual choice is not important, what decision she comes up with is not important. She tells Frank 'What's important is you have brought me to this stage in my life where I can have the exercise of choice and I did not have it before'. (Gill, J., p. 41)

W.R.   'There's a line in the Paul Simon song *Hearts and Bones.* "The thought that life could be better is woven indelibly into our hearts and our brains." It's what my plays are about, the thought that life could be better. I am not interested in how life could be better. I am not interested in whether Rita goes to her mother's, has a baby, finishes her course, or goes to Australia. I am interested that she has got to the point where she can look at those alternatives and feel that she has choice. That for me is the triumph of Rita.' (Jones, C. N., p.335)

Do you see...?
The play can also be seen as having a wider, more political message. One critic says:
"Like most good popular theatre, *Educating Rita* is an optimistic piece and it is inclusive enough to appeal to wide-ranging audiences. Although it cannot be described as a play that advocates political empowerment, it certainly has the capacity to suggest the importance of education as a tool for working-class emancipation. Furthermore, by creating an accessible play that essentially sees the play from Rita's working-class point of view, it is written to galvanize others to follow her course." (Jones, p. 245)

Another critic also puts Rita's decision into a wider social context:
"What will happen to her? Was she right to persevere with a course that alienated her from her own kind? Given the system's failure to cater for her originality, the answer to the second question must be 'yes'"

("What Rita lost along with the shampoo and sets" in: The Times Higher Educational Supplement, 4 July 1980).

Russell himself comments, "with English class structure the way it is Rita has to be better off for having taken her course of action" (ibid).
Students can also be reminded of the various discussions of class barriers as they worked through the play, especially the quotation from Jones in the notes on A 15, 4.

The Choosing
● Answer
– *Both Liz and Mary were equally good at school. They shared the top position/were joint best.*
– *Both lived in the same type of house, but their homes were different.*
– *Mary's family moved to a cheaper flat.*
– *Mary's father did not let her go to high-school (implicit: Liz was allowed to go).*
– *Today Liz reads library books. She might even still be studying. Mary is married and expecting a baby. She probably does not read much any more.*

8. Liz and Rita

Pick out...
– *Verse 3: The same house, different homes/where the choices were made.*
– *Verse 6: (I) wonder when the choices got made/we don't remember making.*
Both the poem and 'Educating Rita' are about making choices. The poem suggests that people cannot always make their own choices, like Mary, whose father refused to let her go on with her education, although she was

good enough. This meant that she had fewer choices about what to do with her life later on.

Rita could not make her own choices when she was younger either. In her case it was because of the expectations of her environment (schoolfriends, family, neighbourhood). She decided to do the OU course because she wanted more control over her life and better alternatives than the choice of eight kinds of beer (p. 40, ll.4/5). She explains to Frank what the exam meant to her, 'I had a choice' (p. 77, l.4). Because Rita chose to pass the exam she also chose to discipline her mind and give the examiners the kind of answer they expected.

9. A press conference

This exercise helps learners to evaluate the play as a whole. Questions might touch on the individual characters, how they relate to each other, the plot, setting, ending, political aims, whether it is optimistic or at least partly tragic etc. It also shows how much has been understood and whether there is anything which needs further clarification or discussion.

Students prepare the questions in groups of about four. The person who feels most competent to play Russell's part volunteers. It is an advantage to collect the questions before deciding on the 'author' to ensure that everyone participates fully and also so that 'Russell' is better prepared.

10. Your feelings

Students should be given this opportunity to give their own personal responses.

A19
Comparison: Pygmalion, Educating Rita

Rita – a modern day Eliza?

Many of the reviews which greeted the first production of *Educating Rita* described it as a modern day *Pygmalion*. Students should not read the reviews in detail, but should only understand that the comparison was made.

After a brainstorming session, students order their ideas as suggested in the table. This comparison, of course, only makes sense if students have previously dealt with Shaw's play.

● Answer

Answers will vary. This is only a suggestion.

Eliza and Rita	Similarities	Differences
Social class	– *working class*	
Motives	– *both want to improve themselves*	– *Rita wants to escape from environment, discover herself* – *Eliza happy in environment, only wants better job*
Personalities	– *take the initiative, intelligent, quick to learn, emotional, direct; dialect speakers*	– *Rita more aware of class system*
How they change	– *learn skills, but also existential reorientation: alienation from original background.* – *changes reflected in appearance, name* – *become more self-confident, gain more control over lives, more choices*	– *Rita knew she would become a different person, Eliza did not. Rita aware of what she would lose. For Rita the break is not so complete, still in close contact with relatives. Eliza almost regrets her education, Rita happy when she achieves her aim* – *Eliza retains new language code. Rita reverts to original dialect after brief attempt to speak 'properly'* – *Eliza's choices more limited because of role of women in Shaw's day*

Higgins and Frank	Similarities	Differences
Attitude to pupils		– *Higgins uses Eliza, no personal interest in her, does not appreciate her, ignores her feelings; irresponsible, pleased with result* – *Frank unwilling to teach Rita, appreciates her uniqueness; aware of consequences of own actions, regrets changes in Rita*
Changes in relationship with pupils	– *role reversal: pupils become dominant, teachers dependent on them*	– *Higgins does not see how Eliza has changed until she forces him to. No insight into own behaviour, no real under-standing of Eliza's new position* – *Frank: self-doubts from beginning, but Rita makes him even more aware of own situation*
Structure of plot	– *women demand lessons* – *fail test half-way through* – *identity crisis* – *woman gain insights, more control over lives* – *role reversal* – *quarrel* – *open ending*	
Themes/ Authors' intentions	– *position of working class people can be improved by education, if they are willing and able* – *moving up in society does not only mean learning certain skills, but involves a complete reorientation* – *different usage of language is recognised as a class barrier* – *class barriers are artificial and can be destroyed* – *education system neglects working class* – *attack conformity, inflexible way of thinking* – *attack complacency*	– *Shaw's play written as a means to an end, Russell's was not (although it also has a political message)* – *Shaw's topic: social and regional dialects; Russell's: the way people talk about literature* – *Shaw targets middle classes, Russell working class* – *Russell targets academics and the 'litera-ture industry'.*

By exchanging their lists students eventually arrive at
a common one which is written on the board or
OHP. This could then form the basis of an essay.

Bibliography

Playscript

Russell, Willy: Educating Rita. Samuel French, London 1981.

Russell, Willy: Educating Rita. Diesterweg, Frankfurt/Main 1997.

Russell, Willy: Educating Rita. Longman Literature 1991.

Video

Educating Rita. Screenplay by Russell. Produced and directed by Lewis Gilbert. Acorn Pictures Ltd., England 1983. Starring Michael Caine and Julie Walters. Available from:
- Lingua Video Medien GmbH, Ölbergstr. 27a, 53639 Königswinter
- Rank Film Library, P.O. Box 70, Great Western Rd., Brentford, Middlesex, TW 89 HR;
- ELT Verlag Lederstr. 21, 22525 Hamburg.
- Fast Forward Units 9/10 Sutherland Court, Moor Park Industrial Estate, Tolpits Lane. Watford, Herts. WD1 8SP, England. Tel.: (09 23) 89 70 80; Fax: (08 23) 98 62 63.

Selected bibliography

Chambers, C./Prior, M.: Playwrights' Progress. Amber lane Press Ltd., Oxford 1987. An analysis of post-war British drama. Russell is one of a group of playwrights whose aim is to broaden the class basis of the theatre. They concentrate on regional rather than mainstream theatre and write about class for working class audiences.

Debusscher, Gilbert: "Educating Rita" or an Open university "Pygmalion". In: Communicating and Translating. Essays in Honour of Jean Dierickx. Debusscher/van Noppen, Brussels University 1985, pp. 303–317.

Gill, John: Willy Russell and His Plays. Countyvise Ltd., Birkenhead 1996. An extensive interview with Russell covering his dramas, his social background and his political intentions. Also includes descriptions of all his plays and a comprehensive bibliography.

Glaap, A.-R.: Willy Russell: Educating Rita. Comments and Study Aids. Diesterweg, Frankfurt/Main 1984. A short collection of comments and study aids on Educating Rita and a lengthy interview with Russell himself.

Jones, Christopher N.: Populism, the Mainstream Theatre, and the Plays of Willy Russell. UMI Dissertation Information Services. Ann Arbor, Michigan 1989. An analysis of the relationship between popular theatre and contemporary mainstream British theatre, with Russell as a representative of the former. Includes an extensive interview with Russell.

Picture credits

p. 15: Flyman & Firkin, British Tourist Authority, Frankfurt

p. 17: John Stillwell, dpa, Stuttgart

p. 25: aus Connexions, His and Hers. J. Groombridge. Penguin 1974

p. 28: "Punch"

p. 34: Mauritius, Stuttgart

p. 36: Catherine Ashmore, London

Weitere Titel zur Unterrichtsvorbereitung

ENGLISCH

Sekundarstufe I

Arbeitsblätter
Englische Grammatik
5./6. Schuljahr
43 Arbeitsblätter für einen
kommunikativen Grammatikunterricht
ISBN 3-12-927874-5

Arbeitsblätter
Englische Grammatik
7./8. Schuljahr
34 Arbeitsblätter für den
kommunikativen Grammatikunterricht
ISBN 3-12-927875-3

Arbeitsblätter
Englische Grammatik
9./10. Schuljahr
32 Arbeitsblätter für den
kommunikativen Grammatikunterricht
ISBN 3-12-927884-2

Arbeitsblätter
O. Wilde, The Canterville Ghost
A.C. Doyle, The Speckled Band
40 Arbeitsblätter mit didaktisch-
methodischen Kommentaren
ISBN 3-12-927885-0

Sekundarstufe II

Unterrichtsideen
Textarbeit im Englischunterricht
der Sekundarstufe II
Didaktische Kommentare und
methodische Anregungen zum
Themenbereich
Cross-cultural Encounters
ISBN 3-12-922694-X

Arbeitsblätter
Willy Russell
„Educating Rita"
19 Arbeitsblätter für einen handlungs-
und produktionsorientierten
Literaturunterricht
ISBN 3-12-927893-1

Arbeitsblätter
G.B. Shaw
„Pygmalion"
16 Arbeitsblätter für einen handlungs-
und produktionsorientierten
Literaturunterricht
ISBN 3-12-927892-3